Don't Just Make A Sale

...Make A Difference!

Jim Doyle

Don't Just Make A Sale ...Make A Difference!

How Top Achievers

Approach Advertising Sales

InstantPublisher.com

ISBN 1-59196-882-8

Jim Doyle and Associates
7707 Holiday Drive
Sarasota, FL 34231

(941) 926-7355
FAX: (941) 955-1114

jimdoyle@upgradeselling.com
WEBSITE: www.upgradeselling.com

Table of Contents

To my children, Brian and Cassie

I will never get a more incredible gift!

∽ઉ

Acknowledgements

I never planned to write a book. But I always wanted to write the acknowledgements! I know, with great humility, that everything I have accomplished is because of the wonderful teachers in my life. That started with my parents, Tom and Dorothy.

First bosses are critical in your career. You will be blessed indeed if you have any like Bruce McGorrill, Don Powers, or Ron Frizzell. I had all three! All are powerful teachers whose lessons still live with me and are reflected on these pages.

I started Jim Doyle and Associates with no clients and little experience (and NO associates!) That's why those very first clients were such difference-makers. My deepest gratitude goes to Alan Cartwright, Lew Colby, Pete Kozloski, Pierre Bouvard, Marilyn Fletcher, Jay Asher, Larry Gilpin, Wayne Daugherty, Joe Reilly, and many more. Also to Linda Rosenberg, Sonja Farrand and Biff Niven who got me started working with Cable folks. Caroline Wilkins gave me my first big showcase at NAB 100+, the speech that made our business.

I am so grateful to all leaders of our TV and Cable clients who have given me the privilege of working with your AE's. You and your teams have taught me so much. Every conversation, every email and every dinner has been a great opportunity for me to learn. I am very grateful for your support and your friendship.

These last few years I have been really lucky to work side by side with a group of amazing men and women. When my long-time friend, Elizabeth Barrett, joined our company as our Marketing Director, my life and our business changed. I could not do what I do without Cheryl Miller, Ruth Schnur and Patti Batten. They are so incredibly dedicated to me and to our clients. Special thanks to Jeannette Cagle who has made this book project and dozens of other projects become reality.

Among my biggest teachers these last few years have to be Don Fitzgibbons and Dave Burke. They are Senior Consultants for our company and difference makers for our clients, but they are also friends, coaches, and mentors, occasionally providing me with a nudge.

A special thank you goes to the men and women who are members of our Achievers Circle. I started this program for AE's, who are driven to be the best, because I missed the day-to-day involvement of watching people get better. The interaction with this group, through the call-in days, tele-seminars, and weekly emails has been one of the highlights of the last few years.

This book is dedicated to my children, Brian and Cassie. I have never received any gift that even comes close to the joy of being their father. They make me want to be a better person every day.

I have been blessed to have four very special teachers in my life over the last 20 years. I am deeply grateful to David Clough, Jim Buckley, Pete

Bissett and Frank Monaghan for being my guides on the adventure that is life. I can never say thank you enough.

Finally, my love and gratitude goes to Denise. I started saying WOW during our first dinner, now I say it every single day. I am so lucky.

Jim Doyle
Sarasota, Florida
December 8, 2004

INTRODUCTION

The title of this book comes directly from a lunch comment made by Milt Maltz. Milt was a hugely successful broadcaster. While he made millions as the founder of Malrite Communications, which first owned radio and then TV stations around the country, Milt was first and foremost a sales person. He started his career selling radio for a tiny station in Michigan, and even after achieving huge success, would still be taking notes at sales seminars - another ingredient of an achiever.

"The problem with our business," he said, "is that we don't have enough sales people who truly believe their mission is to make a difference in their client's business."

Making a difference. The true, customer-focused sales people see their job that way. Sure they love to sell; love the thrill of the chase and the victory, but they understand that true success in our business occurs when their clients win. And, if their clients win, they will get the chance to work with them for a very long time.

Since 1991 I have been training sales people and speaking to their clients all over the United States and Canada. I have had the chance to study - up close - the very best Account Executives in our business. I have found, without exception, that these stars are truly driven to make a difference with their clients. They are much more than customer focused. They are intensely driven to be 'difference-makers.'

This book came out of the weekly email messages I write to the members of

6

my AE coaching group, *The Achievers Circle*. Each week I sit down to write these stars an email that is intended to make a difference to them and their careers, as well as to help them make a difference for their clients.

The subjects of the weekly emails go off in a lot of directions. You'll see some of that reflected in this book. We talk a great deal about what makes advertising work, because the desire to make a difference is useless without that capacity. Wanting to help isn't enough. That's why top achievers in our business are almost always students of marketing and advertising.

Much of what you read in this book is about getting better at selling. How can you make a difference for your clients if you don't know what they need to accomplish?

Obviously, a lot of what we write about is the attitude and behavior of great sales people; about how they set goals and about the attitude of service.

"To get what you want, help others to accomplish what they want."

If you just want to make money selling advertising, then focus on just making sales. But if you want a fulfilling career, filled with incredible opportunities and lots of personal AND financial rewards, make a difference. So start reading this book and start thinking about how you approach your clients.

Stop just selling advertising
and begin making a difference.

The Ingredients Of Your Successful Career In Advertising Sales

The Parade Of Mediocrity

It is a phrase I have only recently used: *The Parade of Mediocrity*. It describes my opinion about how most clients see the advertising sales people in their life.

One year ago, while helping a friend re-position his dealership, I had a chance to work with several AE's who were selling me. If you had listened in on those conversations you would have been embarrassed by the state of our business. There was one person who was the exception. The rest were really very poor. What caused them to be poor? They were clearly more focused on *their need to make a sale* than on anything the client needed.

In Larry Wilson's book, *Stop Selling, Start Partnering*, there is a powerful line…*"When I help others get what they want, I get what I want!"*
Some of the greatest sales people I have ever met spend a high percentage of their time trying to help their clients get what they want. And when they do that, those sales people get what they want, with abundance.

Are you part of the parade of mediocrity? Do your clients see you as being a real asset? Do you give a damn about their business?

**"When I help others get what they want,
I get what I want."**

What Does It Mean To Be An Achiever?

What are the characteristics of the people who have achieved great things in their lives, their relationships, or their careers?

One characteristic has to be the relentless pursuit of knowledge, but not for knowledge's sake. Achievers want knowledge so they can get an *edge* - something that will help them be just a little better. In fact, mega consultant, Dan Kennedy, says there is a group of people who can't stand the idea that there might be good information they don't have, something that could make the difference in their business or their life.

That's why Achievers tend to be readers and tape junkies. I am always excited when I get into an AE's car and they have a CD or tape series in the player, (and I'm *really* excited when it's one of mine!) I also find that Achievers will return again and again to material they think is valuable.

Another ingredient to an Achiever is a vision. They have a clear idea where they are headed. I believe that many Achievers actually visualize their achievements long before they have happened. Think things will be bad? They become bad. Think things will be good? They become good. That's called a self-fulfilling prophecy.

But having a vision means little if that vision isn't reduced to the action steps needed to make progress. Write down your goals. Or, as Marshall Sylver says, *"Write down your PLANS."* He says that plans are more powerful then goals. Think about it. What is more powerful? If I say *"My GOAL is to have dinner with you on Saturday."* or *"My PLAN is to have* *dinner with you on Saturday?"* Which do you think is more likely to happen?

Achievers take their longer-term vision and write down what they need to do next to accomplish it. I think writing down your goals (plans) may be the most critical step towards being committed to action.

Lou Castriota, Jr., a Local Sales Manager at a TV station, was in the audience for my speech in San Antonio. At lunch, he sat down at my table, asking questions about what I thought were the best sales organizations in our business. I was impressed. He certainly exhibited Achiever characteristics. I didn't know the half of it. Lou moved to Harrisburg from a job at a TV station in Baltimore because he had a vision. His vision was to build a center for special needs children that would serve as a model for the entire country as a place where multiple disciplines of treatment could be practiced. He calls this center, *Leg Up Farm.* Moving to Harrisburg, the state capital of Pennsylvania, was critical because it allowed him more access to state decision makers.

Lou has a dream. His dream is to create a program in which horses are used for a therapeutic riding program. His daughter, Brooke, was diagnosed with special needs and from his experience with Brooke came the vision for *Leg Up Farm.*

The farm hasn't been built yet, but it will be. I have no doubt of that because of Lou's determination to see it built. In the past few years, there have been setbacks. Three separate times the grant money was turned down. Then they finally received approval. A woman donated the land, a part of her farm, to build the center. The state approved the use of tax credits for donors. The town approved a change in the zoning to allow *Leg Up Farm* to be built. Now Lou and his supporters wait (and lobby) for a major appropriation from the state budget. When it comes, *Leg Up Farm* will be built.

It's taken years from Lou's original vision to get to this point. Years! And the center is still not built. They've experienced set backs, and may again. But Lou was very clear when he talked about how they have been able to get to where they are today. ***"Stay totally focused on accomplishing just the very next step."*** Lou said it would have been impossible if all he thought of was how he was going to get the farm built. So he stayed focused on the next step. Get the first grant – incorporate - get charitable IRS status - find the land - get the zoning. Take the next step.

Here is a guy just like you and me. He's even in our business doing exactly what we do. He and his wife were dealt a real challenge with Brooke's condition. He has turned that, one step at a time, into a program that will make a huge difference for other children like Brooke. What is your bet? Will *Leg Up Farm* be built? I'd bet huge money that it will.

A dream…a vision…the next step always...action.   An Achiever.

What is your passion?

What do you want to accomplish?

What is your next step?

Have you written it down?

I often ask people who run successful sales organizations – businesses other than the advertising sales business - "What characteristics do most successful people have?"

Usually, the answers don't surprise me. As many of you know, I do a presentation called *The Five Characteristics of Top Achievers.* Most things I hear dovetail with the characteristics I talk about in that presentation. Two week's ago, I asked that question of a friend who is a highly successful ReMax real estate franchise owner. What are the characteristics of the best real estate sales people you know? His answer was totally different than anything I ever had on my list. He said there are two things that distinguish his top Achievers:

1. Humility   2. Discipline

Obviously, I asked for some elaboration since these were words that were not on my personal list. What he said made a tremendous amount of sense to me. I'd like to share it with you.

#1. Humility. My friend said that one of the characteristics of all the top people he knew was *never developing the attitude that they knew it all!* His top achievers are always open to different ways to be more successful. They never stop learning.

I can tell you with some certainty that I believe this observation to be extremely true. In the 12 years that I have been doing seminars, I have come to a very powerful conclusion. Training never takes bad people and makes them good. Training takes good people and makes them great. A seminar's biggest impact is made on people who were already good when they arrived at the seminar. The sinners don't come to church, and the below average performers don't come to seminars (*even when they are in the room!*) If you're reading this book, you have clearly indicated that you want to learn more and get better.

#2. Discipline. Each one of us knows the right things to do and each one of us occasionally does them! An Achiever does the right thing more consistently than others. My real estate friend said that his top people were not always the best salespeople or the greatest communicators, but they showed up every single day, and performed the activities they knew they must to make themselves successful. They did them every day.

I've talked about the distractions we get in our business:
>   …managers want us to sell a special program
>   …traffic and billing systems change and we have
>   to spend hours at the computer as a result
>   …we have a family or personal challenge
>   …a major client needs something instantly
>   …production screws something up.

Doesn't the list go on and on and on? Our life is loaded with distractions. In fact, it's probably safe to say that most of our jobs are filled with distractions every single week. It is so easy to lose focus and stop doing what we need to be successful. The true superstars don't do that. They get distracted just as often as you and I, but after the distraction ends, they quickly get back to what they feel they must accomplish to succeed.

What are the disciplines required to be successful in our business?

16

#1 – Relentlessly doing new business

#2 – Doing things each week or month to build the bridge to the economic buyers of your KEY accounts: thank you notes, articles, and the small gestures that separate you from the parade of mediocrity

#3 – Practicing a formal UPGRADE effort

#4 - Delivering an extraordinary degree of customer service – going above and beyond

Isn't it easy to lose sight of a couple disciplines on that list? We find ourselves running around town preparing for the holidays, signing annual deals, and pitching the special January package.

But, the real achievers do all of those day-to-day activities **and complete** the important actions they believe will lead them to success - <u>every day</u>.

Two words… ***Humility and Discipline***

Spend a few minutes thinking about the greatest sales people you have ever met. What makes them so effective?

I'm convinced they are so totally customer-focused that they believe their role is to make a difference in each customer's business. In fact, great sales people are more focused on *making a difference* than they are on *making a sale*. Consequently, because of their customer focus, they really make a difference and they make *lots* of sales.

Want to make a difference? Here are some ways to start.

1. Be totally focused on getting results for your clients, knowing that when they win, you win.

2. Dedicate yourself to acquiring knowledge. It's hard to make a difference if you don't understand marketing, advertising, and business. Difference-makers are avid readers and students. If you are truly out to make a difference, you have a moral responsibility to give good advice to your clients. This requires an ongoing search for a better understanding of how to produce results for your clients.

3. Spend most of your selling time in diagnosis. Difference-makers don't have to close early and often. They are so aware of their client's needs that they propose solutions and opportunities based on the specific needs of each client situation. That makes closing a lot easier.

4. Think long-term not short-term. You make a difference when your client is more important to you than the next sale.

Difference-makers are <u>not</u> social workers. This isn't <u>just</u> about building relationships. They love to sell, and they enjoy being successful. They are usually intensely driven to win. They study the selling process, but know it is preparation for their real role: to serve their clients and get them results.

One myth about difference-makers is that they are so customer focused they forget whom they work for. Not true. The best sales people know their own company must also win. They actually tend to sell at higher rates because of the greater value provided to their clients. Difference-makers understand that value is not just the spots they sell. It is the total package they offer, which includes the expertise and advice they give to their clients. Difference-makers don't apologize for being paid for that value.

It's not a surprise that many difference-makers practice "above and beyond" customer service. Their clients often tell stories about some unique or special thing their AE has done. For instance, an AE showed up unannounced to help a KEY client with a big promotion, another reviewed all the videotapes a dealership client used in training *their* sales people. It took him 13 weeks to do it, but what a powerful statement it made to that dealer.

Years ago, we tried to get clients to like us. We thought (correctly at the time) people bought from people they liked. Today, it's more accurate to say that clients buy from people they TRUST. Being liked is important, but being trusted is what separates the great from the average. Difference-makers gain a client's trust because the client knows the AE is committed to his or her success.

Now – here's the best news of all. There are very few difference-makers. That means you will really stand out from the crowd if you become one. The implications to your career and your income are enormous. Do you want to be a truly great sales person? Stop making sales and start making a difference.

Successful AE's Build Trust

You almost never see an article in the selling literature about the importance of trust in the selling process. Yet, if you spend time around great sales people and listen to how their clients describe them, trust is very important.

Do your clients trust you? If they do, they'll start to consider you a resource rather than a vendor. They will not only take your advice, they'll come to you for it. You will be well on your way to building the partnership relationship clients will be demanding in the next decade. You will have a far better chance of showing them ideas that can make a difference for their business and they will be open to your suggestions.

How do you build trust? There is no exact formula, but there may be some lessons to be learned from some of the best AE's in the country. Here are some thought starters for you.

1. Do you deserve to be trusted? If you are not worthy of trust, you won't get it. Sound simplistic? It is not. Clients smell phonies. They detest sales reps who fail to live up to their commitments. You will never earn your clients' trust unless they see you as someone who can be trusted. Tell the truth every time. Don't try to bend the rules or play the margins when a client is involved.

2. Do you think about the account --- or only the next sale? The best ad sales people in America are not short-term thinkers. They know that if something is good for the account, it is good for them. They don't worry about the next order as much as they worry about the client's best interests. But guess what? Because of that attitude, they are almost always top billers. They get a lot of orders. One of the greatest benefits of selling advertising is that it is not one-shot selling. Produce results and a client may well be with you for a long time. It's worth your while to think long term.

3. How do you demonstrate your commitment to a client? How does your action compare with competitive AE's who work with this account? Consider the sales rep in New England who showed up unannounced to work at a furniture client's big warehouse sale, or the AE who delivered pizza to a car dealership the night of a special promotion. Leading sales people also show their commitment by continuing to learn. They read everything they can about marketing, sales and their clients. They become a resource to their clients. Travel with top AE's and you will notice that very high percentages are "tape junkies." They listen to educational tapes to get better at what they do. These sellers know that knowledge is power---AND a powerful way to become a big asset to clients.

4. How often do you exceed your clients' expectations? You get credit for great customer service when you do MORE than they expect. Remember to under promise and over deliver.

5. When did you last spend time with a current client on the diagnostic step? Most great AE's do not sell before they determine client needs: it's "Basic Selling 101." Great sales people continue to learn about their clients over and over again. That demonstrates interest. That simple action contributes to a client's sense that they can trust you. In our UPGRADE seminars we often repeat a common expression:

"Nobody cares how much you know
until they know how much you care."

Want to be highly successful selling advertising? Care deeply about your clients' businesses. Be prepared to make a difference. Become a trusted part of their team.

When T.Scott Gross did one of our earliest Tele-seminars for my Achievers Circle, he talked about something that I have always believed. It is called the Law of Reciprocity. It means that if you extend some level of giving, the recipient of the gift will feel some responsibility to reciprocate. Here's an example.

I was considering buying an investment property. I knew the complex and the location in general, but was not able to travel to see the specific unit. The fellow who was selling it to me (who is also a friend) gave me the name of the person who handles the rental program for this complex and suggested I call her.

I called the rental agent and told her I had not seen the unit and wanted her assessment of whether it was rentable in its current condition. Within 24 hours, she had gone to the unit, taken digital pictures of every single room and emailed them to me with some of her suggestions. How much did she impress me? And what is the likelihood that she will get business from me in the future?

Please understand that at this point, I am not an owner who can hire her. I am just a potential owner, but she treated me as if I were an important prospect.

I frequently do a meditation that says, "Every thing I give is given to me in return." The Law of Reciprocity says that if we send service out into the world, we get service back. If we send out frustration, anger and resentment out into the world, we get that back as well. I received a powerful lesson from a real estate rental agent about how true that is.

Power Of Resilience

According to the *Harvard Business Review*, there's a new buzzword for companies trying to find outstanding people. It's *resilience.* That's the ability to bounce back from challenging experiences. There's even a new consulting business helping companies and individuals achieve resilience.

It's a concept that brand new AE's absolutely need. A day of cold calls probably produces more rejection for new sales people than any time since the 7th grade dance. The ability to bounce back from rejection is essential for those AE's who will succeed in our business.

But *resilience* is a key ingredient of success for lots of people, not just AE's. The research says resilient people share three characteristics.
   ✓ **They face reality head on.**
Resilient people may not be cock-eyed optimists. In fact they are realists. They take a real world look at the facts about a situation and realize it may not get better instantly. I have always believed that the sales person who succeeds has a real honest view of the current circumstances he/she is in with a client.
   ✓ **They believe their lives have a deeper meaning.**
This allows them to press on, even in tough times, because they know they are on the way to something important. Concentration camp survivor (and

Psychiatrist), Viktor Frankel, wrote about this in his book, *Man's Search for Meaning*. Frankel believed those who survived the Nazi death camps were people with a vision of the purpose for their life. Frankel visualized himself giving lectures about the concentration camps after the war. Having a bigger purpose allows people in challenging situations to transcend their current circumstances because they know more important opportunities are coming.

✓ **They have the ability to improvise.**

Plan A doesn't work? Try plan B. Resilient people seem, according to the research, to make do with what they have. As the old saying goes *"When life gives you lemons, make lemonade."*

So you ask, *"What does this have to do with me?"* Here's what I believe. All of us will have challenges in our lives. Sometimes big ones: sickness, job loss, a bad work environment, divorce, business failure, and a lot more. Possess two of the characteristics of resilience and you'll survive. Have all three and you'll bounce back quickly.

Every successful person I know (including myself, BIG TIME) has faced challenges. If you are resilient enough to get through them, the other side may just hold your greatest achievements.

I've changed one part of my *UPGRADE Selling*™ training and I believe the change can produce some powerful results for you.

I teach that AE's need to take action every week to build better relationships with their KEY accounts. Everybody agrees with that during our sessions. But do you know what happens? People do it for a week or so, then allow their good intentions to drift away.

I now suggest that AE's make a commitment to take **one hour per week** to build relationships with KEY accounts. Maybe it's the last working hour Friday afternoon or the first hour one morning, but during this one hour, focus on the activities that can separate you from all the other sales people who compete with you.

During that hour you might:

- write thank you notes to Economic Buyers

- send out a few articles

- get your manager to write a formal thank you to a
  KEY account

- think about pro-active actions you can take

- set up an appointment to conduct a *Time Out Call*

If you do that just ONE hour each week, you will be seen as different from all other AE's. You will be taking giant steps to win the trust of your customers. Think this makes sense? **Take out your planner right now and schedule it.** If you put it on your calendar, the odds that you will do it go up tremendously!

Your Mother Was Wrong ...

... when she said *"don't go looking for trouble!"*
If you sell advertising, you *should* go looking for trouble. What do I mean? In our training sessions, we talk about something I call *Optimism Levels*. One of those is called *Fear*. *Fear* exists when expectations are not being matched by performance, or when the client thinks that will be the case soon. Mom was wrong. If you sell advertising, you should absolutely go looking for trouble. And then bring ideas that will fix it.

Mom was also wrong about this!
Mine used to say to me, *"You gotta work hard to get ahead."* I don't know about you, but I've had lots of weeks when I worked hard and got BEHIND!!! It's not about working hard, it's about working <u>smart</u>. Work smart, get ahead, and also get a life.
Here are a few things on my *work smart list.*

- Cut your account list to 45 accounts, active and inactive.
- Spend 1 hour each week doing bridge building (articles, thank you notes) to your KEY accounts.
- Fire accounts regularly when the time= $$$ relationship isn't great.
- Make sure you have a high percentage of *Time Out Calls* that lead to *Presentations.*
- Do new business by category. Go deep, not wide, to become a quick expert in a particular business category. When you sign a new client, ALWAYS ask for more than

enough money to guarantee good results. You'll get a renewal and a long- term client.

Mom was wrong. It's not about working hard. It's about working smart.

Hope Is NOT A Business Plan

One of my favorite clients says, "*Hope is not a business plan*." He sees too many managers and AE's "*hoping*" things will get better, or "hoping" this client starts spending again.

What's your business plan? I beg you to not base it on hope or on hype that the economy is improving.   Fear the worse, and then be wonderfully surprised if it gets better.

Bill Gates used to say, (before the Justice Department made this comment unfashionable), that Microsoft suffered from "*acute corporate paranoia*". Makes sense to me.

Integrity

I have friends who were financially hurt by one of the false, accounting-induced, corporate meltdowns. There seemed to be weekly incidences of top people in these companies walking away with millions. Many people who had busted their butts to build a company, lost pensions, 401K's, most of their wealth and then had to find new jobs. There seems to be a suspicion that all business was done this way. I hope and pray that is not true. I know it's not.

Every one of us has opportunities to shade the truth. I remember as a young(er) sales rep, being asked by a client to indicate that the spots we'd run were for a particular brand so he could collect co-op. I didn't do it. I had a boss who would have been outraged. But one of our competitors did, and got away with it for years. Meanwhile, I didn't get the business. It didn't seem fair!

I've watched AE's use old rating data because it made them look better than the newer info. Some AE's flat out lie to clients or have a quick answer to a client's question, even if they're not sure it's right, in the hope that having a ready answer is the path to a sale. Sometimes the mistakes are mistakes of omission. When I owned a radio station, a tower move was a critical piece to our success plan. A local zoning board was a huge obstacle. So, I conveniently forgot to mention the microwave dishes as part of our application. It was passed. But when they saw the dishes, it opened up a firestorm that was much more painful and more costly than it would have been if I had mentioned it from the beginning.

Short-term gain - long-term pain?

It's pretty easy to lose your integrity in our business. And sometimes, it even seems profitable. Don't do it. It has a huge price.

In sales, I believe we're all self-employed. If you agree, the single most important asset of your personal company may be your reputation.

Even if there is short-term gain, don't ever do anything to damage it. If you find yourself in a situation where a client or a boss asks you to do something you feel is unethical, say no...and leave if the situation persists.

Martha Stewart placed a billion-dollar enterprise in jeopardy because of a decision that made her only $200,000. That's a lot of money to you and me, but a pittance to Martha, who is a billionaire. (She *was* a billionaire until the stock in her company got hammered because of her actions.) Short term gain - long term pain?

I love this: *if you don't want to read about it on the front page of the paper, you probably shouldn't do it.* Debacles like WorldCom, Enron and Adelphia, happened because people (like you and I) made some wrong decisions.

> *It's easy to do, but there is always a price.*
> *even if you don't get caught!*

The Key Issue For This Century
– Time Poverty!

Do you feel busy? Busier than ever? Too busy?
Don't have enough time to get everything done?

You are not alone. Motivational speaker, Les Brown, says that, *"the greatest poverty in the world today isn't in the American ghetto or the continent of Africa. The greatest form of poverty is Time Poverty."*
Consider this:

1) The average American spent 126 hours reading books in 1996. Today it's 109 hours. Total dollars spent on books is up but that's because of higher prices. The number of units sold is down 6%.

2) Women making a major purchase visited 5.2 stores in 1985. Today it's less than 2.

3) The six long weekends are now the biggest shopping weekends for furniture and carpet and other categories. The reason? Women, the most over scheduled of all, finally get a little extra time to shop.

4) Attendance at my three-hour, client seminar has steadily dropped. Attendance from key decision-makers has dropped by an even higher percentage. We've probably done our last, three-hour client seminar and are replacing them with one-hour sessions. I think the three-hour program has more great information for clients, but if they don't come, it doesn't matter how good the information is.

5) I was booked at three state broadcast conferences last year. There was an embarrassing lack of attendance. It used to be that we always had huge crowds at these events. Here's what I think this means to you:

- Selection is an attribute that becomes more important in your client's ad. If I'm going to only two stores, I better find what I want at those stores. Think about this when you look at ads for furniture and carpet. Do they show scope? This is a huge opportunity for TV ads.

- Some retail businesses will plan their ad campaigns around the major, long weekends.

- Everyone will be on the lookout for ways to save time. This could be a key ad benefit for some clients. For instance, a client selling high-end exercise equipment might be in the timesaving business as much as in the healthy-life business.

- AE's will have to be better prepared BEFORE the call. Diagnosis will have to evolve way beyond the *"how's business?"* questions. **Clients don't want to waste their time educating us about the basics of their business.**

- The search for balance will be a big deal for all of us. Who wants to work more hours?

- All of us will have to be vigilant about pruning activities from our life that are redundant.

For the first time ever, I've made a personal commitment to cancel some magazine subscriptions. Internet and email technology gives us an abundance of information; maybe too much information. I'm pruning some from my reading list.

Goals And Lessons

For 20 years, I've been involved in goal setting. I wrote the goals down, left them on my desk and promptly lost the sheet they were on, never to be seen again. One year I actually found the past year's goal sheet when I was writing ones for the New Year. I had not looked at it since writing it.

I had set goals. That's what the success coaches had told me to do. But I'd never looked at them again. So, the fact that some of my goals were accomplished was only a coincidence.

What changed? On a drive from Rochester, New York, to Albany in 1992, I listened to some tapes from Wayne Dyer. Ironically, these were tapes I had owned for several years but had never played. At the time of the drive, things were not going well for me. I had gone broke in a radio deal during the 1990-1991 downturn. I was 8 months into the seminar business and the world was definitely NOT beating a path to my door. I had two young children -- my daughter, Cassie, was just 2 months old. Frankly I was scared.

That day, on Wayne Dyer's tapes, I heard him describe the process he suggested for goal setting. With my radio experience, I noticed that some material had been recorded at a different time and edited onto the tapes. The added material talked about how important it is to review goals regularly. Dyer says review them EVERY day.

The next day, back at home, I wrote out specific goals and put them in a place where they could be seen every single day. And guess what? The results were amazing. I think that everything I wrote down that day came to pass.

Today I believe it's not the process of writing down your goals that causes success. It's programming the mind on a regular basis that makes things happen.

I'm learning (very slowly) it's all about what happens today. If I say I have an exercise program......but I haven't been to the gym this week....then I am deceiving myself. **If I'm not doing it today, then I'm not doing it.**

So, I strongly urge you to write down the goals you want to accomplish this year. You should put things on the list that have nothing to do with making budget or increasing your income. Include personal and business goals.

Then, put the list somewhere visible: in your PDA or planner, as a screen saver on your computer, on the wall of your cubicle, or anywhere that keeps those goals in front of you on a regular basis. That may be a critical step towards more success.

You see, goal setting is only step # 1.

Goal Setting, Part II

Goal setting is the extremely powerful process of programming your conscious mind to move in the direction that you want it to. This subject is so important that we are going to break it into two sections. First, let's talk about the *pre-planning* and *self-reflection* that is required <u>before</u> you write down your goals. Then I will share what I have come to understand about the specific process of <u>writing down</u> your goals.

The old timers in New England say, *"If you don't know where you're going, any road will get you there."*

It is important, maybe even essential, to begin any exercise in goal setting with an understanding of where you are today. Many companies use a strategic planning device that I believe is a great tool for individuals. It is called the *SWOT* method of planning. Simply put, *SWOT*, stands for:

- ✓ Strengths
- ✓ Weakness
- ✓ Opportunities
- ✓ Threats

I urge you to look at each of these areas and with as much self-honesty as possible to see where you stand today. The questions I have posed below are not intended to be the only questions you should ask. Rather, they are examples of the kinds of questions you should be asking in each of these areas.

Strengths:

- ✓ What are you good at now?
- ✓ What are your specific areas of expertise?
- ✓ Are there particular selling skills that you are excellent at?
- ✓ What about negotiation skills?
- ✓ Are you particularly effective in dealing with a certain category of clients?

Weaknesses:

- ✓ How is your time management?
- ✓ How are you at new business?
- ✓ Are you effective at getting to and then communicating with the economic buyer?
- ✓ What about prospecting?
- ✓ Do you do well at selling sports and special events?
- ✓ Are there personal habits that reduce your effectiveness?

Opportunities:

- ✓ Are there new business categories that you might explore?
- ✓ Do you work with clients who have lots of 'glasses'?
- ✓ Would you increase your billing significantly with a planned, focused *UPGRADE* approach?
- ✓ Do you have big events coming up to sell – like Olympics?
- ✓ Should you 'fire' accounts that utilize too much of your time?

Threats:

- ✓ Are there any new, strong competitors for your client's ad dollars?
- ✓ Are there situations where you have no relationship with the economic buyer?
- ✓ Are there category changes?

(An example of this might be what happened this year in the health category. Many states saw changes in Medicaid reimbursement that had significant impact on hospitals and cut hospital marketing budgets. Ford's weakness in sales has reduced the ad budget of many Ford dealers.)

Take some time for honest self-appraisal. Then try to answer these questions:

- ✓ What are the areas of strength where I should be putting more time and effort?
- ✓ Is there a weakness that I should fix?
- ✓ What weakness would have the highest impact on my life if I dealt with it?
- ✓ Should I get organized to take advantage of an opportunity?
- ✓ Are any of the threats I wrote down manageable?
- ✓ If not, what actions should I take to protect myself from these threats?

I believe that all account executives are essentially self-employed. You are Chairman of the Board of Renee, Inc., or Frank, Inc. Your job is to grow your company's revenues. If you were chairman of a publicly owned company and did not use strategic planning, you would not last long. Why then do so few AE's engage in strategic planning for there own businesses? This is only the first step. The next step is to engage in a formal goal setting process. That will be the next chapter. Remember: "Hope is not a business plan." Is it possible that you have placed too much of your success or failure on things over which you have no control? That is why planning is the foundation. It is an essential process that all Achievers need to practice.

Goal Setting, Part III

The process of goal setting may be one of the most powerful activities you can do to program your inner computer – the subconscious mind – to move in the direction of the goals you would like to achieve.

How powerful is goal setting?

If you don't believe me, I would urge you to conduct the following experiment. Go to the five most successful people you know. Ask them what they have done regarding goal setting. I will guarantee you that four of the five have probably gone through some sort of goal setting process. Many of them have formally committed their goals to writing.

One of the most powerful ideas I can share with you about goal setting is this: don't make your goals exclusively professional ones. It would be sad indeed to have all measure of professional achievement, but not experience any joy in the other areas of your life. I urge you to set goals in a variety of different areas. These might include:

1. Personal
2. Family
3. Professional
4. Spiritual
5. Community
6. Health
7. Financial

Here is one way to do that. Write down one thing you would like to accomplish in each of the above seven areas. Use the SMART methodology to create written statements for each of your goals. Each of the letters in SMART represents a different word.

S – *Specific*
Don't make your goal ambiguous. Saying I want to lose weight does not have any power to direct the self-conscious mind. Saying, I want to lose 10 pounds is much more powerful.

M – *Measurable*
Is your goal measurable? As the old management cliché goes, if you can't measure it, you can't manage it.

A – *Achievable*

One of the biggest mistakes I have made in goal setting is to write things down that were unrealistic. When I did that, goal setting became another way to beat myself up, rather than becoming a way to actually elevate my self-esteem. This happened because I set unrealistic goals and then when I did not reach them, I would think I was a failure. Here is an example. If you are making $60,000 annually now, it might not be achievable to make $120,000 in 2004. Perhaps a more realistic goal would be to move to $75,000 annually.

R – *Rewards*

What will you do for yourself when you accomplish your goal? Buy yourself a new outfit - take a vacation - do something special for you. This is an important component of the goal achieving process. Make sure that your rewards are commensurate with your goals. No trips to Europe for losing five pounds!!

T – *Time*

When will you accomplish your goal? This is also very critical. It is another way of dealing with the ambiguity of, *"maybe someday I'll!"*

Over the years I have learned four powerful things about goal setting.

1. **Call them your <u>plans</u>, rather than your goals.** This tip came from motivational speaker, Marshall Sylver. He said it is a more powerful to say I *plan* to have lunch with you on Friday, than it is to say, my *goal* is to have lunch with you on Friday. By changing this simple word, you increase the sense of urgency to accomplish your objective.

2. **As Zig Ziglar says, *"It is a cinch by the inch...but hard by the yard!"*** Losing 30 pounds can be overwhelming, losing 10 pounds sounds manageable.

3. **Write down your goals in a sentence that suggests they have already occurred.** Here is an example.

It is July 1ˢᵗ and I weigh _____ because I eat well and have a daily exercise program.

Lots of people have written extensively about the way the subconscious mind works. Most psychologists will tell you that the mind cannot differentiate between reality and a vivid imagination. To program the imagination more powerfully, talk about the objective as if it has already happened. Everything begins in the imagination.

4. **Review your goals – always.** When I attended my first goal setting program several years ago, I wrote down my goals immediately, stuck them in my desk, and never looked at them again. What happened??? I made the professional goals because I was so passionately driven in that area. But, I seldom made some of the other goals, equally as important, but less at the forefront of my day-to-day life.

Denis Waitley taught me that the process of goal setting has its power *only* when we review our goals all the time. Put your goals someplace where you see them frequently. Write them down in your Day Timer. Tack them up in your office. Make them the screen saver to your computer. Stick them in a book of meditations that you read daily. When you do this, you will program the subconscious mind. "We move in the direction of the things we think about most."

Goal setting establishes your thought patterns only when you regularly take a look at the goals you have written.

Here is my belief. We are all capable of accomplishing so much more, if we apply the same principles of <u>focus</u> we preach to our advertisers, to our *own* lives. The process of goal setting is used by Achievers to outline what their focus is. There is nothing more powerful that you can do for yourself and your success than to review your goals often.

The Power of Self-Talk

One of the single most important books in my life has been **Denis Waitley's**, *Psychology of Winning*.   This is a book that profoundly changed my life. Here's the essence of its message.

We are always moving in the direction of the things we are thinking about most.

Think things will be bad? They become bad. Think someone will like you. They tend to.

Have you ever played golf with someone who, when they got to the short Par 3 hole over the water, reached into their bag and took out an old ball? Why? They don't want to hit a new ball into the water. Their dominant thought? WHATEVER YOU DO...DON'T HIT THE BALL IN THE WATER!!! Where is that ball headed? Into the water, 9 times out of 10.

Waitley calls this SELF TALK. He says that from the minute we get up in the morning, we are always talking to ourselves. Much of our self-talk is negative. *"They'll never buy this." "I can't do that."* If those negative thoughts become what you think about most, your behavior will start to move in that direction.

Here's my personal example. I'll frequently think, *"I'm getting fat."* On the days I am thinking that way, I almost never eat in a healthy way. When do I eat better? It's on the day when my self-talk says, *"You're looking better."* What came first, the thinking or the action? I'd say it was the thinking.

This is the reason that almost all world-class athletes now work with sports psychologists. These professionals help them with the inner thought-process, part of their game. Of course they need skill. ***But if you have the skill and your mind is negative, you will never achieve greatness.*** So what does this have to do with you? You can read the news stories about the economy or the stock market or car sales and you can think things will be bad for you. And you know what? You will be right. *"Whether you think you can or you think you cannot, you'll be right"*.

There is another way to deal with this situation. Some of you have heard me mention Mark Boniol. When I met him he was running the Ford dealership in Shreveport, Louisiana. During the 1990-1991 down turn in the economy, *Mark nearly doubled his store's sales.*

When I interviewed him in 1995, I asked him what he would do if he had read that car sales were heading down. *"I'd throw a party,"* he said, *"because I would be fixin' to get rich."* I still remember him saying, *"When I drove to work this morning, I didn't see anyone riding a bicycle. And I didn't see too many people walking. They're buying a car from somebody. I just have to be sure that it's from me."*

Mark knew a powerful fact. In a time of challenge, most dealers (and most ad sales people) spend their time focused on the 10% of people who are not buying rather that the 90% who are.

I remember that day I interviewed Mark. The camera had been turned off and we were continuing our conversation. He said, *"You know, Jim, if I'm Ford Motor Company and Ford sales are down by 10%, then they are down. But even if Ford sales are down in this part of the country, NOBODY SAID IT HAD TO BE MY 10%! I am perfectly happy if my competitors go down 20% because I am going to be ahead."* Where are Mark's dominant thoughts? In what direction is he heading? **Remember, you move in the direction of the things you are thinking about most!**

Back when I owned a radio station, we had the dreaded Arbitron disaster book. I remember one of my partners asking, *"Has it hurt you more inside the station or outside?"* I had to admit it had hurt us more inside. What had happened? Our dominant thought (ours not our clients) had quickly changed. We suddenly weren't as good as we thought we were.

Here's what I believe. There will be AE's reading this who are having a bad quarter. They will be perfectly happy to blame external factors. It was the economy…I lost that big account…our ratings went down…my boss wouldn't give me the rates I needed to get that order. And do you know what? They will be right…for them. But here's what I know about the winners. They will have the same situation and still find a way to win.

I've talked to a lot of Sales Managers about this. When things slow down the top AE's almost always do a little better. If there's a drop in billing, it affects the middle-of-the-pack players. They tend to make excuses. *Achievers* just figure out a way to make it happen.

I'm not being Pollyanna-ish here. *Achievers* go through tough economies, just like the rest of us. But they change their game plan to adapt to the game they are playing today. They don't spend their time hoping that yesterday's game can still be played.

Several years ago I had a very religious woman working for me. She had a motto I loved. She said, "*I pray like everything depended on God, and work like everything depended on me.*"

So, remember:

- *"We move in the direction of the things we think about most."*
  Denis Waitley
- *"When I came to work this morning I didn't see anybody riding a bicycle. They are buying a car from somebody. I just want it to be me."*
  Mark Boniol
- *"A recession? I refuse to participate."*
  Randy Watson, WTHR TV

"There is one elementary Truth, the ignorance of which kills countless and splendid plans: that the moment one definitely commits oneself, then Providence moves, too. All sorts of things occur to help one that would never otherwise have occurred. A whole stream of events issues from the decision, raising in one's favor all manner of unforeseen incidents and meetings and material assistance which no man could have dreamed

would come his way. Whatever you can do, or dream you can, begin it. Boldness has genius power and magic in it."

Johann Wolfgang von Goethe 1749-1832

Boldness has genius and magic. For me that means, take *ACTION*. One of the greatest things about our business is that we can make it happen. Lots of our clients are retailers who have to wait for people to come to them. We do not. We can make it happen.

How's Business?

I had the most amazing experience at a client marketing seminar in a southeastern market. As many of you know, prior to conducting my marketing seminar, *Prospering in Mega-Competitive Times*, I try to meet as many people in the audience as I possibly can. (As a speaker, I use this device to help make my presentations more "warm calls" than "cold calls.") Last week, within 7 minutes, I met two furniture store operators. I asked each the same question, *"How's business?"*

One gave me a tale of doom and gloom: business was off, the market was soft, didn't think anybody was doing well. The second person said business had been great and gave me specific examples of the near record months they had in the last five months. Both operate stores in the same market. Both deal with the same competitive issues. Both tend to occupy the same price point space in the marketplace, yet one is crying the blues while the other is celebrating.

This reminded me of an old line used by motivational speakers that says, *"Whether you believe things will be good or believe things will be bad...you will be right!"*

Once again, remember Denis Waitley: *"We are always moving in the direction of the things we are thinking about most."* Think things will be good, they will become better.

We really do control our own destiny. The beauty of being in sales is we have the ability to make things happen despite the challenges. I really believe that it is far easier to sell advertising than to run a furniture store. Furniture stores, to a certain extent, have to wait for people to come in, but those of us who sell advertising can go out and make it happen.

What is your attitude? What it is your reality?

Is It Luck?

"Shallow men believe in luck."

Henry David Thoreau

This morning, I was reading a book that reminded me of the old line about the harder I work, the luckier I get. That is so true.

Our company just signed a wonderful contract for training an entire company next year. It happened very quickly. A new CEO was promoted at a company we had worked for 5 years ago. Within weeks we had our new deal. Lucky? Maybe. But I don't think so.

While they were clients, we built relationships with all the KEY decision makers, even ones that did not have final approval over our deals. We did great work for them. Our work ended for their internal reasons. Stuff happens, but doing great work is essential. When the new CEO was considering hiring us this summer, whom did he call? He called the Managers in his company who we had worked with 5 years ago. Even after our formal relationship ended, we continued to treat them as if they were our clients, often sending those managers the memos we were sending to our existing clients.

When the new CEO was named, I immediately wrote a congratulatory letter. I added a handwritten "call me if I can do anything to help" notation at the bottom of the letter. Two weeks later he called me. Just lucky, I guess.

Every week we plant seeds. Some grow quickly. Some take years. Some don't grow at all. You never know which of the seeds you plant this week will pay dividends, and you never know when they will sprout. But, you can be sure that if you plant enough seeds of excellence, your opportunities will grow.

Plant some seeds this week.

Culture Of Blame

As I was dressing in the locker room of our YMCA, I overheard a conversation about a basketball game the night before. I had watched the first half of the game, but had not been able to stay awake for the 2nd half, so I was really curious about the outcome.

"Maryland got beaten by some terrible officiating calls in the 2nd half," I heard one man say. I think to myself, "Wow, I must have missed a great, close game. I should have tried to stay awake"

A few minutes later, I arrived at our office and looked at the paper to read more about the game. Imagine my surprise when I read that Duke won the game by 21 points! It was highly unlikely that a couple of bad calls by the officials caused Maryland to lose. Not when they lost by 21 points!

The locker room comment was only the most recent example I've heard of what I call the "Culture of Blame." It's very easy to find some external reason when things don't work out the way we want them to. I would have been successful (or accomplished this goal or won that contest) if only; my mother didn't drink, if only my co-worker wasn't lucky, if only I hadn't gotten involved with the wrong person.

I see this in many aspects of my life. A member of our son's Little League team was sure nothing was his fault. His mom was quick to tell us about what a teacher had done wrong, or how the team coach had handled him badly. How sad. This boy, at age nine, is already being taught about the Culture of Blame

There's only one problem with the Culture of Blame. It's not true. What happens to me has little to do with outside events. What happens to me is a function of what I decide. I am in charge of what happens to me, not anyone else.

Please understand, I'm not insensitive to the baggage that many of us carry. I know too many people who have been raised by alcoholic parents. And I know that millions of people grow up in disadvantaged environments that give them few of the advantages I have had. But, at some point, no matter what you have had to deal with, you have to decide what happens *now*. In other words, it's NOT what happens to us, it's what we *do* about it that counts.

I call this **personal responsibility**. It's the realization that we have the ability to control outcomes and no external factors can keep us from that UNLESS we allow it.

There are thousands of stories about people with incredible disadvantages who have found incredible success. I read and watched about Wendy's founder, Dave Thomas, following his death. Thomas was given up as a child and was raised in an orphanage for a while. That's obviously why he worked so hard on adoption causes after he became successful. Thomas could have used that as the excuse. The world had dealt him a bad hand. (And it had.) But instead, Dave Thomas took responsibility for himself. You know the rest of the story.

One of the first decisions Achievers have to make is that success is *totally in their own hands.* It has nothing to do with the boss, or the account list you've been given, the economy or whatever. Once you make that decision, start monitoring your discussions carefully. Listen for words of blame. Do all you can to purge blame from your discussions or your silent self-talk. It's not easy at first. The habit of blaming can be deeply entrenched. As long as you let that voice be heard, you won't start to take responsibility for yourself. Blaming is easier. As long as you blame someone else, it takes a lot of pressure off. However, blaming others for your state of affairs is a prescription for mediocrity.

The motivational speakers say it another way.

"If it is to be. . .it's up to me."

What do you want to accomplish in your life? How do you define success? Making that a reality won't be an accident if you stop believing that others are responsible.

In 1997 I spoke at my first CAB conference. It was a defining business event. Within a year, our business had changed. The next year, about 70% of our business came from cable and it stayed that way for about 3 years. Life was good.

Then, 2001, it all changed in a hurry. One of our biggest clients was AT&T Media Services (now Comcast). They had booked nearly 1/3 of our time in 2000. A corporate dictate in January said, *"cut expenses by 10%."* We lost a few dates then. On March 1st, another 10% expense cut, and, with that, about 80% of our AT&T dates were cancelled. While all this was happening, our second largest client, Comcast, went through a change of leadership. Another 20% of our dates were cancelled.

So here it was, March 1st. At least half of our seminars for the year had been cancelled and it was way past budgeting season in a tough business year. 'Stuff' happens.

It is inevitable that you will lose a big account. It's inevitable for AE's and it's inevitable for Sales Trainers. **NO ONE IS EXEMPT. Everyone experiences challenges. But how you handle them is the real hallmark of a champion. Whining doesn't work. Neither does the paralysis of analysis.**

There's only one thing that works: make the calls and increase the selling activity. Make more diagnosis calls – more presentations - more action.

I am proud to say that we replaced every date we lost that year. (I say 'we' because I didn't do it alone.) I also did not play a lot of golf that spring-- we were working. Quite frankly, that wasn't my plan, but the situation changed and I had to change with it.

It's naïve for sales people to think things will ever stay the same. Life is a series of changes. Maybe you're going through some changes right now. How are you responding?

> *"You must do the things today*
> *that no one else will do*
> *if you want the things tomorrow*
> *that no one else will have."*
> **Les Brown**

Memo To The Stars:
How <u>Do</u> You Stay On Top?

Does this describe you? You are one of the best on your team. Your billing has been great. Another year goes by; how do you keep being the best? How do you stay at the top?

A big part of the answer is your attitude; an attitude that says, "I want to be better." As one of my favorite sales managers says, "It's critical not to act like you are number one. Act like number two and you might actually stay number #1!"

I have huge admiration for long-term stars. These are the AE's that not only have become top billers, but also continue to grow their billing and their skills. What do they do? And what are their lessons for you?

Here are some things to look at if you are committed to retaining your star status:

Write down your goals. There is amazing power in the process of writing down the specific things you would like to accomplish in the next year. Writing down goals programs the brain's computer.

Two points on goal setting: Be sure that writing them isn't a singular event. Review them often, maybe every day, and make sure your goals aren't only business goals. I hope your definition of success includes family, community, service, spiritual and education milestones. Write those down as well.

Commit to learning. If you traveled with me for a month or so, you might be surprised to see who listens the most intently during my live seminars? *The Stars.*

Who has various CD programs in their cars? (Your car is what Zig Ziglar calls your *University on Wheels.*)
The Stars.

Stars want the edge. They read more books, listen to more tapes and subscribe to more magazines in order to get that edge. They know that if they stop learning, they stop growing.

Take your service with KEY accounts to a new level. If your biggest accounts had one advertising sales rep at their holiday party, would it be you? Penetrating your biggest accounts is a real opportunity for you to get to another level of success in your career.

I believe that the best among us will have incredible relationships with their big clients. That sounds obvious, but today those relationships will need to be with both the ad agency <u>and</u> with the client. Many AE's have great relationships with the agency, but little direct contact with the client. It is a priority to build strong relationships directly with clients. Stars work hard to get to this point. They write down specific action plans for their biggest accounts and then follow them.

It is a lot more productive to do this when all is going well with the account, than to panic when there's a change because you have no one to call.

Play in a new playground. Make calls in a new business category. Find one with big buck potential, one that requires some innovation and creativity, both in selling and in the advertising solution. There's nothing better for breaking out of your comfort zone, than venturing into something different from the same old, same old. One AE I know does mega, thousand dollar vendor campaigns with manufacturing plants in her market. Another has decided to prospect (and has done so successfully) with Doctors and Doctor-owned clinics. It's great to work in a new category where the formula is different from the norm. It gets the motivation juices flowing.

Raise your sights. If you are a Star, don't work for crumbs! Find clients who can spend a lot. Drop some of your smaller accounts, especially if the time/earnings ratio isn't great. Look at effort expended vs. billings to determine which accounts to drop.

Most importantly, *ask for more money from your existing clients.* Don't call flat year-to-year spending a victory. Make sure your best accounts continue to grow.

Here's a question I ask the best AE's:
"What's the most money you have ever asked a client to spend?"

Take a look at your own history. Why not make a decision to blow past that number at some time in the next 6 months?

"Wing it!" won't cut it anymore.
Sometimes, with a little experience, we start to take short cuts. But the truth

be told, <u>real</u> Stars are going in the opposite direction. They are becoming more thorough, more prepared.

I believe that preparation is key to becoming a Superstar. The most successful AE's are going online before meetings to do some research. Because they do, they are asking better questions, getting deeper into the challenges and goals of their clients. They are writing presentations that take more time and effort and, because of this effort, their closing percentages are sky-high and their average client spends a lot more.

It's said that almost all of the accidents in mountain climbing occur on the way down the mountain. Why? It's when climbers tend to relax a little, lose their concentration and not pay close attention as when they were climbing. Nothing fails like success.

So what's the answer? Keep raising the top of the mountain, so that you haven't peaked. Where is <u>your</u> new peak next year? To stay at the top, don't think that you have arrived. That's the danger zone.

To The New Person In Our Business

Welcome to the greatest business in America. As a sales person in this business you'll have more fun, get more opportunities, and make more money than you can make almost anywhere else, but for most of the first year, you won't believe that.

The first year in this business may be the worst year you'll ever have. Rejection?! There will be more of it this year than any time since your 7th grade dance! I'm sensitive to this. At my first 7th grade dance, the boys and the girls were on separate sides of the gym. With only 15 minutes left in the dance, the boys met and decided to send one boy over to ask a girl to dance. They selected me. Just a minute later, having been turned down, I was back on the boy's side feeling absolutely humiliated. It was the most rejection I had ever faced, until my first year of selling advertising--and it's much harder to start in sales today than it was then!

I've watched hundreds of people start out in our business. Always, my prayer is that they get through that first year; because after that, it does become fun and a lot more profitable. Here are some of the things you can do to become successful in this business:

1. Become a sponge, and find a teacher. I was lucky. I had a boss that really enjoyed sharing this business and took the time to do it. Find a co-worker, boss or someone else to be your mentor. Listen to their lessons and read everything. My favorite people are those who come and hear me for the 5th or 6th time and take notes!!! They come expecting to learn something and they do.

2. Start by making friends. You'll be doing a lot of cold calling. Some of your co-workers have forgotten how to do that. You'll be doing it non-stop. Rather than having an attitude of *"I've gotta sell something"*, just go out and make friends. When you meet people, have a genuine curiosity for their business and their challenges. One of the best Sales Managers I know used to tell new AE's, *"Just go out and make friends. Then make money."* What a great way to approach the first meeting with a client.

62

3. Learn the power of diagnosis. If you've had any training at all, you've probably heard that great sales people usually don't try to sell anything when they meet a client for the first time. They try to determine needs. I believe that if you can master this step of the selling process, you can be a star. Hint: don't walk in cold. Before you meet a client go to their web site. Visit any resources (TV-B, RAB, CAB, Media Center) that can give you some background on their industry. The better your questions, the more valuable information you'll get. This is much more than just *"how's business?"*

4. No matter what the client says on the diagnosis call, go back and ask that client to buy. If they say, *"I hate you...I hate your product...and I don't have any money"*, go back anyway and say *"I know you said you hate me, etc... BUT I had an idea."* You'll soon discover that: 1) most AE's don't go back and 2) this will give you practice for the client where there is an opportunity.

You think I'm kidding? I'm not. The best advice I can give a new person is to go back. Even when you think they'll say no, go back. Don't ever say "no" for your client. Give them the privilege and pleasure of doing that for themselves.

I believe that we have made a mistake in the way we train AE's. We spend some time teaching diagnosis--and it is a critical selling skill. But we fail to stress that there are no commissions paid for diagnosis calls. You get paid only when you sell something. And you sell something only when you ask. Do this for one month and you will have an experience all of us who sell have had. Someone you are convinced will say *"no"* will buy. Don't say "no" for the client.

5. Realize that there may well be a time when you decide you hate this business, or be thinking that you'll never be good at it. Most people who are successful get some of their self-esteem by being good at something. When we are new at anything, we go through a period feeling like we're all thumbs: getting lots of rejection, seeing others doing well, seemingly effortlessly. We are not having success, get discouraged, and start to sour on the job.

Please note; some of the most talented people I have ever hired didn't make it past this phase. These feelings caused them to quit. Once I hired a sales rep for the radio station I owned in Rochester. She had sold high end, very expensive copiers in a major market before moving to Rochester. Her previous boss told me she was *"the best sales person he had ever hired."* After 4 months working with us, she told me she was ready to quit. *"I can't do this."* I told her that she was going through something that lots of successful people have gone through, kept telling her that she was a major talent and begged her to hang in there. It's now 12 years later and she's a VP of a major ad agency, handling their biggest account.

6. Decide that your personal mission is to make a difference in the business of your clients. You will be great in this business if you decide to make a difference, not just make a sale. Make a difference… not just make money.

7. Don't ask for crumbs. I beg new AE's to do the cold calling math.
- **20 calls lead to 6 Diagnosis Meetings**

- **6 Diagnosis meetings lead to 4 Presentations**
- **4 Presentations leads to 1 Sale**

What's the commission on that one sale? Calculate all the time it took to make that one sale and you have worked for minimum wage OR LESS. In our business, selling gets profitable only when you start to get repeat orders. **AND YOU WILL NEVER GET REPEAT ORDERS IF YOU ASK FOR CRUMBS THE FIRST TIME!** You must ask the client for enough money to get the frequency that drives impact. If you don't, *your client loses and you lose even more* because they will not come back. Don't ask for crumbs. Do the math.

There you go. Seven tips to help new AE's get through that tough first year. There are plenty more, like enthusiasm, and using success stories, but those seven are my biggies. Share them with a newcomer. Let's not lose talented people from our business because of what they face in the first year.

More Advice For A
New Account Executive

Last week, I received an interesting email from someone who was new to selling advertising. He had joined our industry at a very young age (22.) He asked for my advice specifically because he felt people perceived him to be too young and inexperienced. I thought you might be interested in the response that I gave to him.

What a great question. And one that brings me back, since I was one of the youngest ever to sell TV when I started at age 22. My first thought is to take your weakness and turn it into strength. Rather than try to pretend you are something you are not, which seldom works, own it. Early in a Time Out Call you might say...."You can probably tell I'm young (then laugh). That's why I ALWAYS take lots of time to find out about the challenges a business is facing. That way I can be certain to do the best job possible for my clients. Because I'm just building my reputation in the ad business, I can promise you I will work harder than any rep you have ever seen."
Then do it!

When making a presentation always credit someone else with the thinking behind your ideas. Rather than say, "What you should do is use fewer glasses," why not say, "Last month, we had, a nationally known, marketing consultant, in town and here's what he said about how a business like yours can increase advertising impact."

Actually, I suggest all levels of AE's use this 2nd party endorsement technique to avoid "telling" in their presentation, but it may be even more powerful for you.

66

Serve people like crazy. Send more articles than anyone in your market. That builds trust and credibility. Prepare a reference sheet with current clients. ("You can tell I'm new in the business, so I wanted to give you a list of some of my current clients. You might ask if I have done a good job for them.") They won't call but it will give you credibility.

Be what you are. And turn it into your strength.
Hope this helps.

Field Mice VS Antelopes

Here's a powerful way to look at your life. I read this in James Carville and Paul Begala's book, *Buck Up, Suck Up and Come Back When You Screw Up.* The story was actually told by former House Speaker, Newt Gingrich (I never thought I'd be quoting him!)

"A lion is fully capable of capturing, killing and eating a field mouse. But it turns out that the energy required to do so, exceeds the caloric content of the mouse itself. So, a lion that spent its day hunting and eating field mice would slowly starve to death. A lion can't live on field mice. A lion needs antelope.

Antelope are big animals. They take more speed and strength to capture and kill, and once killed, they provide a feast for the lion and her pride. A lion can live a long and happy life on a diet of antelope. The distinction is important.

Are you spending all your time and exhausting all your energy catching field mice? In the short term, it might give you a nice, rewarding feeling. But in the long run you're going to die. So ask yourself at the end of the day, "Did I spend today chasing mice or hunting antelope?"

If you're honest with yourself and the answer is mice, you'd better reassess your focus, get back to the strategic core and get your butt on the trail of an antelope."

Who Packs Your Parachute?

On his last day before his early retirement, William deTournillon, KCBD-TV, Lubbock, President and General Manager, sent this out as a thank you to a lot of people he felt had made a difference in his success.

Charles Plumb was a U.S. Navy jet pilot in Vietnam. After 75 combat missions, his plane was destroyed by a surface-to-air missile. Plumb ejected and parachuted into enemy hands. He was captured and spent 6 years in a communist Vietnamese prison. He survived the ordeal and now lectures on lessons learned from that experience. One day, when Plumb and his wife were sitting in a restaurant, a man at another table came up and said, "You're Plumb! You flew jet fighters in Vietnam from the aircraft carrier Kitty Hawk. You were shot down!"

"How in the world did you know that?" asked Plumb. "I packed your parachute," the man replied. Plumb gasped in surprise and gratitude. The

man pumped his hand and said, "I guess it worked!" Plumb assured him, "It sure did. If your chute hadn't worked, I wouldn't be here today."

Plumb couldn't sleep that night, thinking about that man. Plumb says, "I kept wondering what he had looked like in a Navy uniform: a white hat; a bib in the back; and bell-bottom trousers. I wonder how many times I might have seen him and not even said, 'Good morning, how are you?' or anything because, you see, I was a fighter pilot and he was just a sailor."

Plumb thought of the many hours the sailor had spent at a long wooden table in the bowels of the ship, carefully weaving the shrouds and folding the silks of each chute, holding in his hands each time the fate of someone he didn't know.

Everyone has someone who provides what he or she needs to make it through the day. He also points out that he needed many kinds of parachutes when his plane was shot down over enemy territory - he needed his physical parachute, his mental parachute, his emotional parachute, and his spiritual parachute. He called on all these supports before reaching safety.

Sometimes in the daily challenges that life gives us, we miss what is really important. We may fail to say hello, please, or thank you, congratulate someone on something wonderful that has happened to them, give a compliment, or just do something nice for no reason. As you go through this week, this month, this year, recognize people who pack your parachutes.

I offer you this as my way of thanking you for your part in packing my parachute.

You Can Make
More Effective Sales Calls

Win Your Client's Trust

We interviewed four extremely successful dealers for our satellite conference. Over a period of three weeks, I spent a lot of time with those tapes. I was struck by how each of them talked about their opinion of advertising sales people. It was frequently negative. They seemed to be convinced that most of us don't really give a damn about their business.

They each also talked about the few they really connected with. They were consistent in talking about how important it was that the great AE's communicated with them. As Ford Dealer, Rich Klaben, said,

> *"They call me <u>before</u> I call them. If something goes wrong*
> *with a commercial, they are on top of it and telling me*
> *about it. I don't have to call them."*

I continue to sing this song, but I am convinced that we <u>must win a client's trust</u>. Ask yourself what you have done this month to do that. Have you written the thank you notes, sent some articles, or gotten credit for something positive you have done for a client? Doing all those things helps win the battle for trust, which will help you gain some ability to control what is happening with that account.

How Important Is
ATTITUDE In Selling?

It is everything! I've seen lots of very effective sales people who do not have great product knowledge or selling skills, but they have wonderful attitudes. Conversely, I know a lot of sellers who know the product cold but are not effective on a call. **Talking about selling without talking about attitude is like talking about the Atlantic Ocean without mentioning water.** What are the specific attitudes that Achievers have? I think there are three.

ATTITUDE #1.

Great sales people have an attitude of service. They are genuinely customer focused. How can I make a difference in your business? That's the question I find lots of great sales people asking. They know that if something is good for the client it will ultimately be good for them.

They also know that the single most customer-focused thing they can do for a client is to make sure their advertising works. They study (relentlessly) how advertising works on their medium. And they are quick to reject ad schedules they believe will not produce results. They stay consistent with that philosophy EVEN if it's the end of the month and they are a little short of budget.

This pre-occupation means they produce results more often than other sales people. Therefore, their repeat business is far, far higher. That's one of the main reasons they bill more.

Please note: The attitude of service is backed by the desire to learn how to get results for clients. It is not enough to be a caring person. You express your care with your commitment.

In the past few years, I've learned that what I give away comes back to me. As I serve others, I get back even more. And the more I give the more I get back. Want a life of abundance? Give more.

ATTITUDE #2. Curiosity

If you asked me why I was great at sales, this would be one of the biggest reasons. I genuinely liked the Time Out call process because I loved learning about a client's business.

After about three years in sales, I recall being asked how I liked my job. I said it felt like I was getting an MBA in Small Business Management. What a gift to get an inside look at how hundreds of small companies advertise and market. I don't know how it would be to feel I <u>had</u> to ask those questions. It might feel like an unpleasant task that I had to get through quickly. I have the opposite problem (as those who have made calls with me can attest). I can't stop asking questions.

For most Achievers, that curiosity also causes them to be voracious readers and students of business. Many of you have heard me talk about Dave Melville. Dave was one of the best AE's I've known. If I mentioned a book at a seminar, Dave wrote it down. And by the time I was back (a month or so later) he had not only read it, but he'd probably given two or three copies to clients he thought might enjoy it.

(As for myself, I read *Forbes* EOW, *BusinessWeek* weekly, 5-6 weekly broadcast and cable trades, 3 daily fax newsletters or E Zines, *Wall Street Journal* several days weekly, *USA Today* Money section daily and 3-4 business and/or motivational books each month. It's amazing how often I'll read an article that helps me on a Time Out call. By the way, I've read at this level for over 27 years in the business. Read like you want to be a CEO and you'll be able to talk with any you meet.)

ATTITUDE #3. Enthusiasm

The best description of enthusiasm I have ever heard came from the coach of the first Women's Olympic Basketball team. She said that in her opinion the last 4 letters of ENTHUSIASM, I-A-S-M, stand for "I AM SOLD MYSELF."

Something powerful happens when you deeply believe in the power of your product, or the power of the ideas you are bringing to a client. When you believe ....deeply,......it comes through in the confident way you present your ideas.

One of the best sales managers I have known used to tell his AE's, "If you're not RED HOT, how can you warm up a customer?" He believed that selling was a lot like putting a pan of water on the stove. No matter how hot the burner got, the water would never get as hot. That's because when energy is transferred, some energy is lost. I think selling is another form of transferring energy. If my burner is set on LOW when I head out to sell, how HOT can I get my prospect? Not very!

Enthusiasm does not necessarily mean the jump-on-the-table, "I'm GREAT" rah, rah of seminars (although that works for some). It's the powerful force you transmit when you believe deeply.

Three attitudes:
Service, curiosity and enthusiasm.
Combine them and you are on the way to achievement.

Attitude: Be There!

I just read an interview with Lindsey Wood Davis. Lindsay was Executive Vice President of the Radio Advertising Bureau. (He's now a partner in a radio group.) He's quoted as saying, "I used to teach my salespeople that there were three things they had to get across on a call.

1) I'm happy to be here,

2) I know what I am talking about and

3) I love my job."

When I read that I went "Wow!" When I think of all the really great sales people I know, they do all three.

My former client, Milt Maltz, (former because he sold his company, Malrite Communications, told me he thought the problem with AE's was that not enough of them saw their role as "making a difference in their clients' businesses." Milt, who started selling radio at the proverbial 1000-watt day timer, believed that the secret to success was to show up with a genuine desire to make a difference. And if you did that, you would be very successful. (One aside about billionaire Milt: he sat through my entire afternoon sales seminar -- and TOOK NOTES!) Making a difference in the business lives of your clients - that's the essential key to Lindsay Wood Davis' first two points.

1) I'm happy to be here and 2) I know what I am talking about.

I also think that the concept of making a difference is what drives many of us to be knowledge junkies. I have always wanted to know everything I could possibly use to better serve my clients.

Lindsay's third point "I love my job" is huge. We want to buy from people who are excited about the power of their product. I've written about the last four letters of enthusiasm standing for "I Am Sold Myself". I think it's essential to spend a few minutes before every presentation making absolutely sure you are convinced and, most importantly, why?

When I was writing these ideas, I remembered one other quote. Max Dixon, one of the leading coaches for professional speakers, says, "Show up ready to be no place else." In other words, be very excited about being exactly at this place, at this time. I see some speakers who seem to be half-present, giving the impression they have done the speech a few too many times. I hope I never get that way.

Max's quote reminds us to be completely *in the moment*. Don't be in the middle of a speech, or a sales call, or time with your kids and be thinking about the next day or the weekend. Be present.

Show that, as Lindsay would suggest, *you love your job!*

78

Graham Stone sells TV advertising in Lethbridge, Alberta, Canada. He's a member of our Achievers Circle. He and I have developed an email friendship. It's fun for me to hear how TV is sold in Canada.

After one of our teleconference calls, Graham sent me an email that I thought was great. He raised a good point and he said I could share it.

"Jim, thanks for the conference call today. I got on shortly after it started...had to attend the grand opening of our first The Home Depot this morning.

The Home Depot is already on our station and will buy through our national sales office in Toronto. When I saw 9 key product areas The Home Depot was selling, I realized I may not get a local buy from them, but there's a wealth of opportunity for me to target other businesses who sell water heaters, garage doors, cabinets, electrical products etc. Even better, I can get one on one with the person who can make a local decision and who doesn't have to check with someone in another city who may think of my station/market as a low priority in their big-picture marketing scheme.

One consideration is that some of them, like the Furnace Duct Cleaning guy, may not be called on by ad reps (except yellow pages) because of a low profile address, usually in an industrial park. I heard a funny comment in a seminar one time. The person said "Don't you wish those yellow page reps had psychic powers like us. We know who <u>not</u> to call on and who <u>won't</u> buy, *but yellow page reps just don't seem to get it. So they call on every business on every street!"*

Your line about go deep (or go home) in a category is so true! Thanks!

Graham Stone, Global Television Lethbridge

Alberta, Canada

A very good sales organization with a culture that is totally focused on selling is Comcast in the Philadelphia market. Where has Comcast recruited a large number of their AE's? You guessed it; The Yellow Pages. In general, successful Yellow Page sales people have a tremendous work ethic, love to sell, and are constantly trained to have an UPGRADE mentality. Personally, I believe that the next wave of training in our business will feature a return to basic selling.

And Then, Go Deeper.

I was talking about new business development at a management program. Lindsey Wood Davis was in that audience. I was talking about my advocacy of the *"dig deep"* philosophy for new business. This is the concept of doing new business by category, so that you can learn more as you dig deeper into it. Lindsey said that I might take that one step further. He said, *"The University of Wisconsin Medical Center has 82 separate profit centers."*

Think about it: 82 people who have a budget to make; 82 different marketing challenges. There is a second part of the digging deep philosophy. That is to look at the opportunity in different areas or departments of your existing accounts.

Does the service manager have an ad budget? Is there another area of the bank that needs to be marketed?

Go Deeper!

Prospecting From The Curb

Our Senior Consultant, Dave Burke, is developing his own seminar on *"Back to Basics"*. He shares my belief that many in our industry need to get better at basic selling skills. His program looks great and he was showing me the outline Saturday when a line jumped off the page.

"Don't prospect from the curb!"

Dave thinks many AE's decide on the potential of an account without ever speaking with anyone. They *prospect from the curb* instead of making an appointment.

When I ran the radio station in Rochester, we had (for us) a big account that was a clothing shop in the garage of the owner's home. (It was a big and remodeled garage, but a garage nonetheless.) She gave us thousands of dollars. She had tons of co-op. Most AE's would have driven by again and again because she didn't look like a big business. They were *prospecting from the curb*, and they were wrong.

I bet that almost all Achievers have a client like the one above, one whose spending would surprise their competitors, one that few AE's would even bother with.

There's another version of this lesson. One of my favorite Sales Managers used to say, *"Don't say 'no' for clients. Give them the privilege of saying no for themselves."*

Isn't it true? A new package is introduced at the sales meeting and we think *"They'd never buy that."* What have we done? We've just said no for the client. I promise you have clients who would cheerfully buy programs or promotions you've never presented because you thought they wouldn't.

How do I know that? It's because some of the largest sales I have made were when I believed there was no chance of a sale, even as I walked into the call.

Two great lines. . .
> *"Don't prospect from the curb."*
> *"Don't Say NO for the Client".*

The <u>Real</u> Decision Maker

I've had a bunch of meetings with car dealers in the last month and a half. Most of them use an ad agency, but took the meeting with us.

What does that say to you?
What it says is that even when dealers have advertising agencies, they are highly engaged in their marketing. Advertising is in the top three expense categories for every dealer. They are perpetually questioning what's working and what is not working.

I promise you that these dealers' agencies have very little control over what is going to happen at that account. These meetings continue to make the point that it is *essential* you have a relationship with the economic buyer. That is true of all accounts, but especially true for car dealers.

Send thank you notes, have your manager call, send articles regularly, stop by on a Saturday to introduce yourself. Do the things that no one else will do and you will have impact

Getting Your Voice Mail Messages Returned

My colleague, Dave Burke, sent me this. It is very powerful.

"I was at a convention a couple years ago and went to a session about how to get through to unreachable clients. The speaker there was a big area advertiser. He showed us how he treated voice mail. (He actually had a phone hooked up and played back messages for our illustration.)

Each one started the same way: "Hi, Bob, this is Dave from WABC. I have..." That's all we heard before he hit the delete button. The next message was the same: "Mr. Jones, this is Mary with WXYZ. Our station..." DELETE. He said unless he already knew you and/or was doing business with you, the message wasn't even listened to. He didn't have time to hear 30, 40, 50 messages a day. He couldn't listen to them all, even to discern if any of them had value. It's sad, but true.

Here's what he suggested: give him the meat up front before you identify yourself. That way, you have a chance of intriguing him before you get deleted. So, the message might sound like this: "Hi Bob. We're having incredible success growing sales for businesses like yours here in Albany. I'd like to show you how we can drive traffic for you and drive your competitors crazy. My name is Dave Burke and I'm with WABC. Call me back and I'll come right out with specific information about how we can do the same for you. My number is 333-3333. Thanks a lot!" If nothing else, you've gotten past the "delete" button and have a better chance of catching his interest."

Again, no method works all the time, but if you're having trouble getting noticed, try this and see if it works for you. *Good luck!*

Great Opening Lines

Here's a way to get a first meeting started and could also be a powerful voice mail. Very few things sales people say should be memorized or scripted. But, there is one time when you should have a line you can nail 100% of the time. (This line can also be used to get appointments over the phone.)

It is essential in the first few seconds of meeting a new prospect that you accomplish three things. You need to tell them:

1) why you are there

2) what's in it for them

3) that you are not going to try to sell them anything!

Years ago, we developed the following opening line to say very quickly after getting in front of the client. Here it is (and I have memorized it!):

"Let me tell you why I am calling.

At _____ we have worked with a lot of businesses in this area and have produced some extraordinary advertising results. But, frankly, I don't know anything about your business or your situation. What I would like to do is spend some time with you to discuss the issues and challenges you are facing and see if it makes sense for us to work together at some point."

Use this line to tell them what this meeting is about, give them some incentive to stay (*we have worked with a lot of businesses and produced some spectacular results*) and take away any fear that you are going to try to sell them something today (*so we can think about whether we should work together at some point down the road*).

If you use this approach, it will help you do better Diagnosis Calls and increase the number of Diagnosis Calls that you take into Presentations.

Several years ago, we measured the *UPGRADE* efforts of several clients and compiled monthly reports. Here is what we discovered.

Many sales organizations reported lots of *Time Out Calls*, but few *Presentations*. For many AE's, the *Time Out Call* had become a customer service device. Let's visit with this client, find out how things are going and learn how to do a better job of serving the client.

The high achiever never uses the *Time Out Call* as a customer service device. The *Time Out Call* is the beginning of a *selling process*. Achievers do *Time Out Calls* with the expectation that it will lead to a *Presentation*. And, while that sometimes does not occur (for a variety of reasons), it is always their goal.

As we speak with sales people, we have found it is not uncommon for many to conduct the *Diagnosis Call* and not return. Why do we not go back? It is usually some kind of fear; fear of rejection, fear of acceptance, or fear's second cousin, procrastination.

In the early 90's, at the start of my training business, I had a prospecting system. I phoned potential prospects and introduced myself to them. My sales presentation often went like this...

"I am calling to introduce myself. I would like to send you some information about what we do and call you again in a few weeks to talk about it further. Would that be OK?"

Frankly, almost everyone agreed to have me send information. Ten days later, I had to decide what to do on this sales call day. Call more new people? Or, call back the people who had received information. My choice, more often than I care to admit, was to call more new people. It was easier for me to call them because there was no rejection. As I watched my savings account balance get smaller, I realized that I was not calling them because of fear they would say *no*. So, by not calling, I was *guaranteeing* that I got a "no." Today, I believe *I can only get a yes if I am prepared to hear a no.*

This is profoundly powerful. You will NEVER make money in sales by being great in diagnosis, even though being great at diagnosis is a critical selling skill. You will make money in sales only if your *Diagnosis Calls* lead to Presentations. So here is the question:

What *Diagnosis Calls* have you made in the last three weeks that should be followed by a *Presentation* this week?

Write the *Presentation* and call to schedule the appointment!! Here is a suggestion from our most successful AE's. They book the return *Presentation* at the conclusion of their *Diagnosis Call*. Once they have the appointment, it's far harder to procrastinate. I strongly believe that this is an important part of the selling process.

A Powerful Diagnosis Idea

If you've heard our *live* UPGRADE Selling™ seminars, you know we believe that the diagnosis step is the critical part of the selling process. We call our diagnosis call a *Time Out Call* to convey that this call is not just for a new prospect. It's also the call you make with someone with whom you've worked for a long time. It's your opportunity to be sure you and your plan are current with the issues going on in their business right now.

In the last few months, I've been talking about something in my *live* seminars. In the earliest part of the *Time Out Call*, I urge AE's to ask about the client's business. The questions in this section are more extensive than the *"how's business?"* questions. Find out about strengths, not just in sales, but also in:

1) Profit and
2) First time visits.

We have stressed for a long time that AE's need to discover what contributes most to a client's sales. Remember, if 70% of your cases are car accidents, you are a car accident lawyer. Analyzing the client's strength often suggests the appropriate marketing strategy.

What if the strength of their business wasn't especially profitable? If you suggest a client spend money to promote something they don't make money on, they are likely to resist your advice.

Case in point: A New Jersey music store gets 75% of their sales from guitars and 25% from Keyboards. Yet, Keyboards represent *75% of their profits*. The music store would appropriately reject any advice to make them into New Jersey's Guitar Capital.

Here's another question to ask. *"What do people buy when they come into your business for the first time?"* Here's an example. The client is a "Wild Birds Unlimited" franchise. 60% of their business is bird feed and feeders. 40% is accessories; books, videos, pins, et al. At the holiday season, the owner wanted to advertise accessories. Makes sense right? Especially for the holidays? Well, it didn't work.

I was asked for an opinion. I asked the client this question. *"What do people buy the FIRST time they come in?"* Guess what? 90% of the people who come in for the first time come in to buy either bird feed or a bird feeder. Who buys the accessories? It's people who have already been there to buy bird feed or feeders.

If the AE had asked this question at the beginning of his diagnosis, he would NEVER have had the client run ads promoting accessories. It's a campaign guaranteed to fail. And worse, if they really want to grow their accessory business, the fastest way to do it is to grow the bird feed and feeder business. When the client grows strength, their weakness often improves as well. Ask clients what customers buy on their first visit. Often that's what you should promote.

Dave Burke says he always asks about what he calls *"the point of entry"* during his Time Out Call. This is the first purchase people make at a business that we just mentioned.

This is powerful and worth repeating. Businesses waste millions trying to stimulate sales of products that are bought after the customer has come in for the *"point of entry"* product.

I recently consulted with a nursery chain. Their point of entry was flowering plants, annuals and perennials. They had a big business in fertilizer, mulch and chemicals and spent thousands to promote them. Who buys that? It's mainly people who come in for flowering plants.

This nursery chain had a gift business. Gifts represented a significant piece of their business. But who bought gifts? First time gift-buyers discovered gifts when they were there to buy (no surprise) flowering plants.

So, apply the James Carville principle (It's the Economy Stupid!) and you say, *"it's flowering plants stupid."*

If this nursery spends almost all their ad money to promote flowering plants, they will stake a far more powerful claim in the market. Flowering plant sales will go up, big time. And here's the kicker, so will sales of fertilizer and gifts. Ask the question about point of entry in your Time Out Calls. And remember the marketing lesson.

The Lee Bickford Question

One of the greatest salespeople I ever worked with was Lee Bickford. Lee had a knack for closing business for BIG dollars. Here's one of the things he did....

When he was finishing a diagnosis (Time Out Call) with a new prospect, Lee would ask them a question. He would say, *"If I could bring you back an idea that you thought would make a huge difference in your business, could you spend $ _____ between now and the end of March?"*

One day, after making sales calls with Lee, I asked him how he came up with that number. He said, *"I take the biggest number I think they could spend and I double it!"* He did that because he had frequently understated what the opportunity might be.

What was Lee doing with that question? He was putting a bigger number out on the table right at the *beginning* of the conversation. You would be amazed at the number of times the client responded by saying that they could spend that number. When they said they couldn't, he would ask them for the amount they could spend. And, that number was still higher than one might have expected.

The challenges with *New Business:*

It takes –

-20 Cold Calls to get 6 Appointments

-6 Time Out Calls to get 4 Presentations

-4 Presentations to get 1 Sale

If I then ask the client for a small amount of money, my commission on that is tiny. I have worked for less than minimum wage. There is only one way that *New Business* pays off for us--when you get the 2nd and 3rd order. That's when your hourly wage goes up dramatically. But, most AE's lose the opportunities to get the 2nd and 3rd order because they ask for so little on the first go-round.

If clients don't "fill a glass" the first time, <u>they will not get results.</u> If they do not get results, they will not renew. The Lee Bickford question helps put a number out on the table that is *BIG* enough for them to see the power of your product.

It is a powerful question!

Not Everyone Wants A Consultant

When I was a sales manager, I was frustrated by a VW dealer who bought our competition each month but did not buy us. Finally, I decided to handle the account myself. Here is what happened:

Month #1 – I called on the dealer, did my *Diagnosis* and brought back a suggestion for a higher frequency approach than the three spots per month they had been buying in my competitor's 6pm news. They listened politely, thanked me for my interest, and a few days later booked a three spot, 6pm news schedule with our competitor.

Month #2 – I went back to them again and articulated how important I thought frequency was. I outlined the way I would accomplish it. The result? They booked an identical 3 x 6pm news schedule with my competition.

Month #3 – I sold them three spots in our 6pm news. The lesson? I tried to begin every relationship by being customer focused and by trying to be their consultant. But, not every client wants to buy that way. Unfortunately, they call the shots.

So, what is the answer? We can continue trying to be their consultant and explaining the right thing to do. I might be right, but, I will have a moral victory with no commission to spend. There are some situations where clients do not want to engage in your process. And, it's OK.

We have to do business the way our clients want to do business. Until we build trust, we won't change that.

Not everybody wants a consultant and not everyone who needs the advice wants it. That is sometimes a hard lesson to learn.

Three Critical Diagnosis Questions

As you all know, I believe the best AE's are relentless at *Diagnosis*. They are constantly working to determine the needs of the client.

I also believe that the entire reason to build a relationship with the *Economic Buyer* is so they will let you, at some point, conduct a *Time Out* (Diagnosis) *Call*. Here are three questions that will help you find out what is really going on with your clients:

A) The Magic Wand Question
"If you could wave a magic wand and change anything about your business (or your marketing) what would it be?" Another version of this is to ask what about their business keeps them awake at night.

B) Next Year's Expectation
The Question: *"What do you expect sales in your industry to be next year?"* *"What about your company's sales?"* Try to get them to be specific. The answers tell you a great deal. What will happen to their ad budget if they

think their sales will be dropping? What will happen to the budget if next year is stronger?

This also helps determine their *Optimism Level*. Is your client *Optimistic, in Fear*, or *Don't Rock the Boat*? Once you can figure out their *Optimism Level*, you can begin to determine how to customize their proposal. If you've forgotten about *Optimism Levels* or aren't using this tool often, I encourage you to revisit that section on your *UPGRADE Selling™ Audio Library*. It is extremely powerful.

C) How much do you spend?

Are you asking this question every time? I hope so, because the client will answer almost every time. The amount they spend will almost always be *MUCH* more than what you thought. In fact, if you want proof that a client's impact diminishes as they spread their dollars in too many places, start asking about their ad budget in detail. You may find yourself saying, *"They sure are INVISIBLE for that kind of money!"*

As most of you know, I believe this single question may be one of the two most important parts of my initial *UPGRADE* training. Asking this question causes AE's to *raise* their sights a lot! So many times, we go into the *diagnosis* thinking we are doing very well with a client. But after asking the question, we may discover we are getting crumbs.

There are some AE's who don't ask the question. Why? It's usually their fear or the mistaken belief that clients would consider that question prying or too personal. All I can say is that clients are telling us. They might be telling your competitors--and they'll tell you, <u>if you *ask*</u>.

One more thought on *Diagnosis*. During your call, start timing how long it takes before you ask the first advertising question. The <u>longer it takes, the better.</u> Make this about *their* business, their customers, their competition and their plans and you'll have a far more productive call. What's more, the client will actually think you give a damn.

Projects Or Partnerships

"We're being barraged with all the little projects they want us to sell. Doesn't that contradict what you're telling us about how to grow our business?"

The project mentality seems to be permeating sales organizations. If you allow it, this can take you off your *focus* as an AE. And, by the way, it also causes your manager to lose focus as well. Many sales managers complain about all the corporate crammed-down projects they are being told to sell.

AE's are asking *"Aren't we creating the perception of being the dreaded peddler with all the stuff we are supposed to be selling?"*

Since this question is raised so frequently, here are my observations.
1. There are too many projects. We are asking AE's to keep too many balls up in the air.
2. You and I won't be able to change it. It's the reality of the world in a challenging economic environment.

97

Here's why it happens. Everyone, from the corporate CEO down to you, wants the same thing. They want to grow the business. Corporate big shots have other pressures as well. Maybe pressure from their bosses....or to make the debt payments....or to keep the stock value strong.

Under pressure, people look for quick answers (remember in the training we talked about when people go into *"fear"?)* They have a far higher sense of urgency. Their goal becomes FIX IT NOW!! They believe the way to fix it is to get their AE's selling more projects. They hear of an idea that has worked in one market and, presto, there's a mandate it be sold in every market, regardless of how many other initiatives are on your plate. This is not going to change as long as business is weak. If anything, it might get worse.

How do you deal with this project mentality without being seen as just another Peddler by your clients? You must have a *diagnosis-first* mentality in the selling process.

I write so often about *diagnosis* because I believe it is the one skill that separates average AE's from the stars. I believe in doing diagnosis (Time Out Calls in our system) non-stop. I do *diagnosis* when meeting a client for the first time. *Always. No exceptions.*

I do *diagnosis* at least once a year with clients I'm already working with. That's the first step in a potential UPGRADE effort. And I do *diagnosis* when I've got a package or promotion to sell and think a certain client might be perfect. First, I learn more about what's happening with that client. Then I can come back with a customized selling approach that shows how my product can help them solve *their* problems.

AE's with a *diagnosis-first attitude* can sit in a sales meeting and think, *"I've got a home for that idea."* because they know their clients well and know which ideas will work for which clients.

When I go to sell the package, I *customize* my selling approach to show how this package/promotion/value-added can help them with an issue in their business. Approached this way, the promotion part of my proposal is Customer-Focused. It helps my billing because I can get some clients excited about an idea that works for them. Everyone wins.

But what can cause you huge problems and have your clients label you as the dreaded "peddler"? Take all the different packages out to the same clients all the time. This week you've got one idea, next week it's another. That becomes the selling equivalent of throwing a lot against the wall and hoping that something sticks. What sticks? Your clients see you as just another sales person and not someone who really understands their needs. You hurt yourself.

It's important to the team that all AE's sell what managers put out. Their bosses are asking our managers about it. Everyone is under a lot of pressure.

One of the reasons you to do new business calls continuously is to get more prospects for the next idea or package your manager asks you to sell. It's possible to be a great Customer focused AE and win all the awards and contests for selling the 'packages'. In fact, it's essential if you want to be one of the best.

Start with a *diagnosis-first attitude*. Only offer people the ideas that can help them. Don't pitch all your clients every idea. When you do that, you may make fewer presentations than some of your co-workers, but you'll sell just as much because your closing percentage will be much higher

Meeting Client Expectations

Do you have a clue what your clients' expectations are? Years ago, I heard a sales trainer say that every time we close a piece of new business with a client we should ask that client,

"What do you expect to get from this?"

If they expect to sell 20 cars and you know in your heart that they've bought a 3-car schedule, you need to know that, right then. You can either increase the schedule or turn the business down. Otherwise, they will be a disappointed, non-renewing customer.

As I've said, getting a business on the air the first time is an incredibly inefficient use of your time. New business pays off when clients renew. But, many AE's don't get the renewals because they UNDERSOLD the client the first time and the results were not there.

A GREAT Selling Idea

I have been around sales for over 30 years. Very seldom do I hear a selling idea that makes me go *"WOW,"* but I got one from Alan Figg, one of the superstar AE's at WTHR.

Alan works with a fast food chain whose agency was frustrating him. Seems they always booked at the last minute. Because of that, they were always paying the highest rates. He had repeatedly tried to convince them to book earlier and pay less. Alan's station frequently gets sold out, so the way the agency was buying kept his share of the buy pretty low.

So what did he do? He found out the name of the Sr. VP of Marketing at the food chain, called him and left the following message. *"I think I have a way to get two free months of advertising for your company."* And guess what? The VP called him back. Alan explained that by booking ahead they would save enough money to pay for two months of advertising. The VP bought the idea and they placed an annual buy. And Alan got rewarded with a very high share of the budget.

In my seminars, I say that we should *"sell the hole and not the drill bit."* The normal pitch I've always used for annuals is *"lock in lower rates".* What Alan did was take that one step further and created a huge benefit for the customer. *"Two months free advertising."* In my opinion, this is 10 times more powerful than *"lock in lower rates"*

Thank you, Alan, for sharing this idea with me!

Making Your Presentations Better

Here are a few quick ideas...

a) Look at your title again AFTER you write the current situation. Many times the current situation describes a business in "FEAR," but the title is more related to an optimistic client. Remember that your title is the KEY piece. It should be specific to a client's situation.

- ✓ *Growing Saturn of_____'s Used Business*
- ✓ *Increasing Sales in the Superstore Era*
- ✓ *Growing Enrollment in the new Competitive Environment*
- ✓ *Maximizing the ABC FORD Opportunity in a Time of Overall Declining Ford Sales*

b) Repeat your title over and over in your presentation. It's easy to keep your template the same or to write your presentation by starting from one you have already done. But, when we do that, we sometimes don't customize beyond the title page and the Current Situation.

Every time the title returns in a presentation it reminds the client of the true purpose of the meeting.

c) Make your Presentations Look Great. Make your client's logo the watermark for the whole presentation. (This looks GREAT!) Or, try using a piece of clip art as the watermark. I just saw this done and it looked awesome. An AE took a great picture of a furniture display and made it the watermark on his presentation to a furniture store. WOW.

Use a picture relevant to the business on each page of your presentation where it makes sense. One AE presented to a restaurant chain. He went to the web and got pictures of their stores from various markets. Then he set up his PowerPoint so that there was a place for a picture. He used it on pages that had his station info and the proposed schedule.

d)   Use Third Party Presenters. What's more powerful? Saying, *"Here's how to make advertising work,"* or you saying, *"We had a nationally known marketing consultant speak to our group and here's what he said it took to make advertising work."* Way more credible.

When I sell, I make extensive use of third party endorsements. This is much more powerful that using the *"I"* pronoun.

e)   Share Success Stories. Most of you know how strongly I believe that success stories of other businesses are the CRITICAL component for sales effectiveness and HIGH closing percentages.

Make your presentations better and watch your income grow!

Have We Forgotten How To Sell?

Lately, I've been wondering if in the Omega/Strata world we live in, is it possible we've forgotten how to sell? Are we focusing enough on selling in our training and in sales meetings?

I'm not talking about diagnosis. As you all know, I think that's the most critical call in the sales process. We emphasize that in all our training.

I'm talking about what happens when you return to the client with a proposal. How do you present your ideas? Is it matter of fact? Or do you get excited? Are you conversing or are you selling? This week when you are out on calls, do a spot check to see how you are doing in three areas:

1. How's your enthusiasm? I don't mean the jump on the chair, *I'm great!* stuff you hear from the motivational speakers. As I've mentioned before, the best definition for enthusiasm I have ever heard is the last four letters of the word ...i...a...s...m ..
"I AM SOLD MYSELF".

Do you believe in the idea you are presenting? I mean <u>really</u> believe. More importantly, do you convey your passion for your idea? Are you sold yourself? One of the best AE's I ever knew wasn't a particularly good presenter, but she wrote business like mad because she got excited about what she was selling.

2. Do you change features into benefits? I should probably write an entire column JUST on this. It's Selling 101, and yet I see presentation after presentation loaded with features.

Here's the short course:
A FEATURE is when the seller says something from their point of view. Ex: "We're #1 with men!"

A BENEFIT takes the same thought and answers the customer's question, "What's in it for me?" Ex: "We'll be able to reach a huge percent of your potential truck customers efficiently because we are # 1 with men."

Big difference. This takes practice. Great sales people are constantly working to get better at this. It will produce a big difference in your selling ability (and your income) because you will constantly think about how every aspect of your proposal helps your client solve their problem or seize their opportunity

3. Do you ask for the order? I've noticed in the last 2 years that a large number of the presentations I'm asked to critique don't use the closing page that we build into our model.

At the end of your presentation you must ask for commitment. Even if it's as simple as "what do you think?"

I believe in assumptive closing, particularly if I have done a great job on the diagnosis step. But even then, I have to say "assuming that everything makes sense up to this point, here's where we need to go from today forward". You must be prepared to hear no in order to get a yes.

And remember, the old rule still applies.

Leave without an order
and the probability that you lose the sale
increases dramatically.

Think Outside The Box

I love the cartoons in *The New Yorker* magazine. I actually had one framed for my office. In it, a casket salesperson is talking to the couple. The caption is:

"We also have urns, if you want to think outside the box."

Thinking outside the box may be one of the most overused consulting terms ever, but I found myself using this phrase when working with many members of our Achievers Circle group. These are extremely successful and experienced AE's. When I was managing sales staffs, I used to tell AE's at this level that they should spend some time doing new business in totally different categories.

We had one AE who targeted major manufacturers for budgets in public relations, community relations and employee relations. We had another AE who worked on business-to-business advertisers.

I encouraged these sales people to call on categories they had not worked with before and, particularly, to call on non-traditional advertisers. These accounts may not have had a cost-per-point, but perhaps had more intellectually interesting issues than the typical car dealership! Better yet, they probably had some money that no one else had tapped.

If you have been in this business for a while and you are successful, I strongly encourage you to spend some of your new-business effort making calls to potential advertisers no one else is calling on. Do these for no other reason than to challenge yourself and expand your horizons by thinking differently – Outside the Box!

How Much Money Should You Ask For?

Advertisers at our client marketing seminars frequently ask how much money they should spend on advertising. Very often, they have been given an accountant's answer based on a certain percentage he or she thinks they ought to spend. In the old days, it was typically 3%. However, in the real world, the answers are often very different. Here are four ways you can look at ad budgets.

Relationship between rent and advertising

If a business pays extremely high rent (say at the big mall), the theory says that one can spend less money on advertising because the location will yield a high volume of traffic. This is an older theory, but it still has validity in many situations.

The cost of not doing anything

At a recent seminar, a client asked me about what they should do if a major national competitor was going to be in their market in one year. My answer: spend everything you can on advertising to build market share now. An old joke goes, "When the elephants dance, the ants take one hell of a beating". When dominant market leaders fight each other, it is the small guy that goes away. So, if you know a dominant player is coming into the market place, it is imperative to grow all the market share you can <u>before</u> they arrive. In this case, throw the accountant's formula out the door, since you need to advertise strategically to insure your future opportunity.

What is the opportunity-cost?

This weekend, I saw an ad for an assisted living center here in Florida. (This is a great prospecting category if you are looking for new business opportunities.) It reminded me of working with one of these facilities a few years ago. That facility was a hundred-unit complex just 6 months old. Forty of the units were empty. The average rent was $1500 per month. Do the math.

$1500 x 40 = $60,000 in lost revenue opportunity.

That is just what they lose in one month! That loss occurs again the next month. How much should they spend on advertising? The reality is they will spend a boatload if you bring them a plan that they have confidence in. That situation is a $720,000 a year problem. I urge you to always calculate the opportunity-cost.

When we bought the radio station in Rochester, it was a dog! It was doing less than $20,000 a month in sales. The first three months we advertised the station, we were spending as much as 200% of our revenue on advertising. Was this insane? Not at all. We were building a brand to establish ourselves in the marketplace.

Many times, start-ups try to advertise their way to success <u>incrementally.</u> That is a long and tough process. If I have a budget for construction because I need a building in order to be in business, why wouldn't I have a budget to build awareness in the market place, since that is even more important. What is it going to cost to be even a small player in a market? That budget should be part of the start up cost of any enterprise.

I hope these thoughts will give you some ideas that will be helpful when a client asks you, *"How much should I spend!"*

"How Much Should You Ask For?"
Part II

Here's an example:

An Assisted Living facility has 100 units available for rent. The average rent is $3000 per unit. When you meet with the client you learn that, since this is a relatively new home, only 50 units are rented. This means 50 units are not yet producing income. What should they spend to remedy the situation?

The math will give you the answer. (You'll probably have a smaller number UNTIL you do the math.)

50 Units x $3000 = $150,000 lost revenue .. PER MONTH.

That's right…this isn't a $150,000 problem. It's a $1.8 Million problem if the vacancy rate extends out 12 months.

How much should you ask for? It would depend on how certain you are that you could guarantee success. They will clearly spend more (and should) than the $5000-$10,000 many AE's think is a big order.

Here's another example: We called on an alcohol rehab in-patient program. There were 35 beds in this unit, but the average occupancy rate was 25. The charge for the typical 28-day stay was $7000. What should they spend? In this case, here's the economic equation:

10 Beds x $7000 = $70,000 monthly revenue lost. This translates to an $840,000 annual revenue loss potential.

Fixing this problem has huge impact on profitability. Since this clinic has already paid their fixed expenses for rent, heat and counselors, much of this extra money could go to the bottom line. They'd spend a lot to fix that problem.

When you do the math with any client where this makes sense, you will find that what they spend now may not be a guide to what they should be spending!

Several years ago, I was with the General Manager of a TV station when we conducted a *Time Out Call* on the *Economic Buyer* of a big bank in their market.

It was a great call. The bank was spending $65,000 with the TV station, but they had lots of issues. As the call went on, I was convinced we could go back with a Presentation and ask for $125,000, maybe a little bit more.

As the call was winding down I heard the GM ask the banker a question. *"If we could put together a whole series of ideas, really build a partnership between the bank and our company, could the bank spend $500,000 next year?"* I was convinced the banker would shoot us. Instead, he leaned forward in his chair and said *"That would be a stretch."* My GM closed a $425,000 sale to the bank 12 weeks later.

As some of you know, I use that story occasionally to close a seminar. I've never forgotten it. Why, I ask, did my client think he was in a $500K meeting WHEN I thought we were in a $125,000 meeting? We were both in the same meeting.

At some point, the amount of money we ask for comes down to our own personal level of belief. Do you believe in the power of your product? Do you believe that if they gave you ALL the money, you could hit a major home run for them? This GM believed that. He believed it from the bottom of his heart. He could argue it passionately. I didn't and I would never have been able to ask for the same amount of money as he did.

"The good is often the enemy of the best". If I had made that $125K sale, there would have been applause - *"Great job, Jim"*. I would have basked in the glow of my big UPGRADE, but I would have left $300,000 on the table because I didn't believe.

How powerful is your medium – your glass? Do you believe, truly believe, that when clients spread out their ad dollars they dilute their potential results? Do you have the belief to ask for all the money?

When The Client Asks, "How Much Should I Spend?"

Maybe there's a different way to look at how much a business out to budget for advertising than the accountant guidelines or the national industry averages, but first, a story.

I work with a consultant, Dan Kennedy. Kennedy helps speakers grow the non-travel part of their business. Projects such as our Sales Manager Boot Camp and our Achievers Circle group are ideas inspired by him. He's been a powerful teacher.

A while ago, we were talking about subscriptions for our *Auto Revenue Insights* newsletter. He asked me, "How much would you spend to get a new subscriber?" Now my belief is we're an aggressive marketer and I know a little about Kennedy's philosophies. So I said, "The annual subscription brings in $197. I'd spend over $100 to get one."

I think I'm being aggressive. After all, that's over 60% of revenue. What business spends over 60% of their revenue on advertising? Kennedy asked me to do some homework and see if my answer might be different after the research. He asked me to calculate how long an average subscriber stays with our newsletter. He also asked me to check and see what new subscribers spend on tapes and other products in the first year of their subscription.

Here's what we learned.

- Our average subscriber is with us about 5 years. (We have huge numbers who subscribed in the beginning and have never left.)
- A new subscriber averages about $200 in purchases in the first year.

So, what is a new subscriber really worth? Is it $197 for that first year subscription, or is it a whole lot more? Kennedy believes that many businesses ought to calculate the lifetime value of a customer.

In the case of our newsletter subscribers:

$197 x 5 years = $985   1st year tapes = $200   Customer value = $1185. Now ask yourself. What would you spend to get that? At what level of spending would that still be profitable? Kennedy suggests that many information marketers should actually go negative to get the first year subscription. (Going negative means spending more on the first order than the first order will cost, knowing that in the long run, the math will work in your favor.) Turns out there are huge numbers of information marketers who will go negative *big time* because they know …to the dollar….what the upside will be.

What should I spend to get a newsletter subscriber, knowing the calculations? Probably a whole lot more than my $100 answer that I thought was very aggressive. Is this relevant to you? I think so.

There are lots of clients who ought to look at the lifetime value of a customer, rather than the national averages for their brands. Here are a couple of examples…

1. A Lasik surgeon sells vision correction in one eye for $2000. The surgeon's hard costs are about $800, so there is $1200 profit. 50% of patients get the second eye done within 6 months, if not immediately. If done at the same time, the hard costs are only about $500 per eye.
Do the math… (I'm guessing on the numbers, but it makes the point!)
- ✔ 50% will have an average profit of $1200 (One eye only)
- ✔ 25% will have an average profit of $3000 (Both eyes at same time)
- ✔ 25% will have an average profit of $2400 (Both eyes, but not at same time)

Average profit per patient is $1950. What would you spend to make that? I believe that an aggressive surgeon might spend $500 per new patient all day and all night knowing that there's a 4 to 1 payoff. Their accountant might think that was crazy but, in fact, the surgeon might be brilliant. This example applies to Lawyers and lots of other professionals.

2. In the 80's I bought a dog radio station with some partners. Billing was only $20,000 per month. We changed format, lost billing at first and spent about 150% of sales on advertising. Why? We knew the lifetime value of that listener would be huge. Get ratings and the ad dollars will follow. (Try to explain spending 150% of revenue on advertising!) But, if we hadn't done that we probably would have stayed a dog station for a long time.

3. A few years ago, an ophthalmologist (that's the MD) came to one of my marketing seminars. He had a problem/challenge. After investing millions in a brand new surgery center, he learned that in 18 months, Medicare would reduce by 40% what they will pay him for cataract surgery, his specialty. He has 18 months to become a high volume player because he must make up for the loss in average patient spending by doing a ton more procedures.

How much would you suggest he spend? Remember, if he hasn't accomplished his goal in 18 months, the rules change and he's got a big problem. So, how much? This was a small market, the kind of market in which $10K per month is a lot. But that's what he spent. And it worked. We would have actually hurt his business, if we had asked for less.

I'm not trying to suggest that every client should significantly increase their spending. I'll be honest. I can't bring myself to go negative in pursuit of a new newsletter subscriber. I am, however, much more aggressive now.

I urge you to start thinking a little differently:

116

- How much should a client spend?
- How big is their opportunity?
- What's the downside?
- How much can they make?

I hope this makes you think. Do me a favor; read this a few times in the next week to plant the ideas more firmly in your brain. You might want to use this kind of thinking on a call, real soon.

How to Make The Campaign Launch A <u>Big Deal</u>

You have just sold a great schedule to a new client. Or, you have gotten someone to *UPGRADE* significantly for next year.

How can you turn the launch of the new schedule into a *big* deal? As many of you know, I love to put on meetings for clients – either at our facility – if it shows off well – or at theirs. We often forget the *magic* that is associated with our advertising medium. I still remember how exciting it was the first time I went into a TV station. You can capture that same excitement for your client's employees when you create some *magic* with the show business of our media.

Why not hold a sales meeting for your client? Come up with a couple of contest prizes. Buy a Fox sport shirt, an NBC sports cap or a CNN premium as prizes. Serve bagels, coffee and orange juice. Have an on-air person come in to say "Hi." Give them a tour of your facility. Make the launch of their ad campaign into a very *big* deal.

Every single business has a second constituency. The first is, obviously, the customers they want to reach with their commercial. But, the second are their internal customers. AE's who help their clients market to internal customers are well on the way to building partnerships with those accounts.

Answering The Question But...

Recently, I received the following email from an AE with an unusual client situation. (I've changed the names to protect the innocent.) The client has a problem, and raises it during a *Time Out Call* with an AE. The AE is trying to solve the problem. That's the way it's supposed to be done, except for one thing. The client is focused on the wrong issue. Read the following exchange and then I'll elaborate.

The Original Email:

Here is a client need/problem that came up during my Time Out Call with ABC Motors. (He has many problems - but this is the one he asked for help/feedback on.) When he loses a local customer sale to the dealer 20 miles outside of town it is because:

1. *Local customers shop their own backyard first*
2. *They get first bid/price from ABC and then drive 20 miles with bid*
3. *After driving 20 miles, the other dealer has only to beat ABC's price by a few dollars and the customer, having already invested a lot of time, gives that dealer the sale*

So, here is the challenge – finding a creative way to reverse that process and get people to shop the competition first and then get the best price from ABC Motors. Signed, *Looking for Ideas.*

Jim's Response:

Regarding your situation....

Every dealer faces the issue that ABC does. You could run a *"shop us last"* campaign that probably will not help much. In my opinion, the focus is wrong. Rather than focus on the customers lost, (which is inevitable), focus on getting more shoppers to come in first. Do that by leading with strength (trucks or SUV's if possible), building a consistent image, having a memorable *"save you a lot"* hook and use "fewer glasses." (Advertise in fewer places.) When dealers get more bang from their advertising, they will draw more traffic and appear to be much bigger. Even if their closing percentage stays the same, they'll grow sales. I'm convinced that as they appear to be a bigger force, their closing percentage should actually go up.

I'd also look at the 'inside the store' process to be sure the *"why buy here"* message is being delivered *powerfully* throughout the sales process. I'd make that a formal part of the process and put letters from customers who saved at ABC in every cubicle, especially letters from people in the area that dealership wants to penetrate. I'd also be sure the dealership sales people referred to testimonials in the selling process.

Several years ago a PI lawyer asked me, *"How do I get more big cases?"* My answer? *"Get more small ones!"* You have to kiss a few frogs before finding the prince. Want more princes? Kiss more frogs. This seems to apply here.

Jim Elaborates:

Two points here…

1. Sometimes clients ask you to solve problems that can't be solved. Could you run an ad and say *"We only want big cases."* Doubtful.
2. Often, the client's focus is in the wrong place.

A grocery chain in the south, owned by people with very strong religious convictions, did not open Sunday nor did they sell beer or wine. I wanted them to mention that subtly in their ads and, without preaching, stake a claim. Take their weakness and turn it into strength. They were afraid that they might offend some people if they did that. Question: if you offend 2 but 50 love you, is it worth it?

Howard Stern is hated by 10x the people who love him. And he's still the number #1 morning show in NYC. It doesn't make any difference how many people hate you, if the people who love you love you <u>with passion</u>.

What's the bigger risk? Having no one love you or hate you; be vanilla and get lost. Too many businesses are worried about the customers they lose, rather than focusing on the ones they keep. That's what ABC Motors should be doing. They ought to know they will lose some and not worry about it.

Here's an idea that can make a difference during a holiday week. Why not spend as much time as you can to just say, "thank you" to your best accounts? Either drop by or call with no other agenda but to say thank you. Get voice mail? Leave a thank you message.

Ask your boss to do the same with your top 3 clients. I believe that the simple gesture of saying "thank you" is so uncommon that it pays huge dividends. I learned this many years ago. In the late 70's I managed a radio station in a medium-sized town in Maine. Every year the owner, Ron Frizzell, and I would spend two full days dropping by to wish our clients Happy Holidays.

The response was always wonderful. It usually is anytime you have an opportunity to engage in a non-selling conversation. For many of our non-retail clients the pace was a little quieter at their business and they seemed to enjoy the break.

Think about it, when was the last time anyone you do business with called just to say thanks?

Two weeks ago, I received a phone call from an AE who is a star! But... this year the star is a little tarnished. A couple of major cancellations have occurred that she had no control over and a couple of other things that she was working on did not come through. Now she feels she is in a slump.

Every AE goes through slumps. It is almost guaranteed that you will have one sometime during your career. How do you pull out of it? Here are some thoughts that might help, if this happens to you,

A) **Don't try to think your way out of a slump.** It is impossible. There is only one way to get yourself out of a slump: sell your way out!

B) **Increase the volume of your calls.** Get out of the office and go see customers every possible minute! Taking action is energizing!

C) **Recommit to a Diagnosis Call.** When we get into a slump, we may start pitching "stuff" and then get frustrated when our clients don't say "yes." It is probably a lot more profitable to go out and redo your Time Out Call. Spend time in Diagnosis to learn about needs. Then bring back solutions to problems.

D) **Work on things that will improve your attitude.** What gets you jazzed? Is it exercise? Is it music? Is it some form of spiritual growth? Whatever it is, do more of it to lift your spirits.

E) Go help someone else! Volunteer at the Salvation Army, Humane Society or any number of other organizations. Do something for someone less fortunate than you are. Sign up to be a Big Brother/Big Sister. When we get "outside" of ourselves, we increase our enthusiasm and confidence. It WILL make a difference.

F) Stay away from people who will drag you down. Misery loves company. There is always someone else in the office going through a challenging time who wants to have lunch and tell you how bad things are for them. Avoid that person like the plague. Instead, spend time with upbeat people who make you feel better about yourself.

Slumps happen to everyone. That is why you might want to bookmark this page and save it for the day you need it. Or, pass it on to someone on your sales staff that may need it right now.

Why Trash The Competition?

I need to share my feelings about some AE's apparent need to trash their competitors. Why do some of us need to do this? I believe that <u>every</u> time I speak negatively about a competitor it diminishes <u>me</u>. If you believe that to win, someone else needs to lose, then you are forced to trash your competition.

But if you believe, as I do, that you can win and others can win as well, then there is no value to being negative about your competition. Remember, a basic premise of our UPGRADE Selling™ system is that all advertising works. *What doesn't work is spreading ad budgets in too many separate places.* That is the principle of the glasses that you all have heard me speak about.

So, no advertising is bad. The only bad thing is using too many separate places. That is the enemy! That is what you ought to be trashing.

Your Strategy When Accounts Have Agencies

I believe advertising agencies have done a lot to help our medium grow. However, I am convinced that most sales people are so afraid of agencies they hurt themselves in the long run.

Today you *must* have a relationship directly with your client when there is an agency involved. If you don't, your billing (and your commission) is vulnerable to a competitor who does have that direct relationship.

Never forget that agencies are not spending their own money. The money belongs to the client; and that client has strong feelings about how it should be spent. In many cases, clients are making the decisions. Ever hear your agency mention the words "client dictate?" Today, great ad sales people adopt an attitude that says "they're our clients too."

Here are some specific suggestions to develop relationships directly with your clients.

1. Build your bridge to the client when everything is great, not when the relationship is falling apart or you've just gotten a cancellation. It's tough to build bridges when the river is on fire.

2. There is incredible power in small gestures. Thank you notes, articles, and other personal touches can separate you from all other sales reps that call on an account. Send these directly to the client and copy the agency.

3. Your manager may sometimes be the person who makes the contact. Managers often like to deal with other managers, but it's your job as the AE to make that effort happen.

4. When you get a chance to speak directly with your client, don't talk about ratings or other "spots and dots" information. Remember that your client is more concerned about effectiveness than efficiency. Their biggest concern is the bottom line. Show them how your product can help improve their bottom line and you are speaking their language. Think ROI.

5. Do not let your efforts building a relationship with your client take anything away from the service you provide the agency. Always give your ad agencies incredible customer service.

6. When the agency has done something that impresses you, tell the client how you feel. Remember, we are not trying to be adversarial with our agencies.

7. If the agency gets upset about your efforts with the client (and they will) ignore it. Blame a higher authority. "I had to. It's a new policy from my corporate office. I'm sorry."

Do these actions make you feel uncomfortable? It made me feel uncomfortable when I first watched my competitor do them to me. I got even more uncomfortable when that same competitor kept getting orders from accounts that were not buying me. I came to understand that, like many sales people, I wanted to be liked. I hated doing anything that would lead to conflict. I finally decided that being liked but not bought is losing. That is not a victory.

Many of us have attitudes about ad agencies that were formed at a time when fewer media choices existed for advertisers. Back then, we could win just by winning the ties. Today, when more and more choices chase fewer and fewer clients, there are no more ties. If you do not have a relationship with your client, someone who does, is going to take your money.

Is it *really* worth it? Maybe you could have a story like this. A Florida AE was getting no business from a car dealer. She had tried and tried with the agency to no avail, so she built a relationship directly with the decision maker. This summer she closed an order for over $200,000!

Are You A Wimpy Closer?

Here's an observation after having critiqued several presentations recently. Lots of sales people don't seem to want to ask for the order. I suggest you close by using a time line in your proposal that outlines the timing on all the next steps. (Copy OK'd, production completed, etc). I am shocked at the numbers of people who leave that part out. YOU MUST CLOSE!!! And this is a good way to do it!

Those of you who have heard me speak know that I do not believe in the hard charging, close early and close often, approach. I believe that most great sales people close assuming they've gotten the order. They ask questions after their presentation just to confirm. Top sales people can do that because of their skill in the diagnosis step. They do such a thorough job uncovering their clients' needs that they assume the solution they propose will make sense.

Here's the deal. Even great sales people say something at the end of their presentation to see where they stand. Even if it's as simple as *"Does this make sense to you?"* or *"Based on what you've heard are you prepared to take the next steps?"* Anything, even "whaddya think" is better than waiting for them to respond.

You don't have to be hard sell to ask for the order. And you'll never be great in sales until you ask for the order, every time. Don't be a wimp!!!!

I am on a *mission.* I want to start talking about selling again. In discussions (many of which I have led) about customer focus and diagnosis, we have lost sight of the basics of sales.

Let's continue the discussion of the most basic concept of all. I beg you, when you end a presentation, specifically ask the client to buy. I like to say something like, *"Let me summarize what we have talked about here."* (Then give your summary with benefit statements and success stories.) *"Now, Ms/Mr Business Sales Person, I need to ask you - does this make sense to you?"*

We <u>used</u> to spend a lot of time in sales training talking about the closing question. This is the last statement of your sales call where you ask a question (even something as simple as "what do you think?"). The closing question marks the point at which it becomes their time to respond.

Years ago sales people were trained to shut up completely after they asked the closing question. In fact, we use to joke that the first person to talk would lose. I'm not sure that is still relevant, but I would strongly urge you to resist the temptation to start talking again if there is some hesitancy to their response. Give them the time to think about their answer – and wait.

What comes out of the client's mouth next will either be an order for you or an objection. If it's an objection, you must try to overcome it. We'll write more about that later.

I am amazed (astounded, frightened, horrified....pick an adjective) by the number of presentations sent to me for critique that do not include a Time Line in the final page. There is only one way you will get a "YES" in our business. That is when you lose your fear of hearing "NO." *Don't be afraid to ask for the order.* Ask every single time you present options to a client. Ask questions as simple as, *"How does this sound to you?"* Your billing will go up.

When Do You Give Up?

Sales people are a group of highly driven people. Most successful salespeople have strong amounts of ego drive. Ego drive is defined as the intense desire to win. Persuading others of our point of view is a great "win" for us.

One of the most challenging situations is having a client who can benefit from advertising with us and has the money to do it, but is totally resistant to change, or, even worse, gives us a small amount of money every year. An AE recently told me she had a car dealer who gave her $10,000 once a year for the big tent sale and nothing beyond that.

Many of the calls that I get during my Call-In-Days are about these kinds of situations. You have done everything you can think of, so you decide to see if Jim has a magic potion. And, you know what? I usually don't.

I believe everyone can be sold, but, also that I will not be able to sell everyone. Someone may do it, but it probably will not be me.

The best decision you can make in this situation is to ask your manager to move that account to someone else. Then, turn your attention to people who want to engage. Turn your attention where there are opportunities. Turn your attention to situations where the time equals commission-potential equation makes sense.

In my conversation with the AE who had the $10K tent sale order, I asked her to calculate what her hourly rate was based on her commission and whether working for that amount of money was a good economic decision. She had called on this dealer twice a month and had spent hours at the dealership.

When she does the time-spent equation, it is likely that she may be willing to give that account up. Although the account is a big spender with other media, they have a strong opinion on how to do things. It may take a long, long time before that client could ever pay off for her. If ever! In the meantime, the time and energy (including emotional energy) she is expending is not made up by the income she can make.

Look at your account list and ask yourself this. Are there clients that I should give up on and move to somebody else?

Love To Sell?

I hope that you had a chance to watch the made for TV movie, *Door to Door* staring William Macy. (It's available at most video stores.) This was an incredibly moving movie for anyone…but particularly for those of us in sales. The movie followed a 40-year period in the life of Bill Porter.

Porter was born with cerebral palsy and overcame all kinds of physical obstacles, including a speech impediment, in order to become a successful door-to-door sales person.

Door to door sales has to be the toughest form of selling in the world. Think how much tougher it is if one has physical and speech disabilities! Yet Porter became so successful that he was, at one point, his company's *"Sales Person of the Year."* At his acceptance speech he said, *"I love to sell!"*

I fear that in our Tapscan/Consultant sell world, we have lost sight of how important it is to love to sell.

Mr. Porter's mother drove him to his first job interview and to his territory each morning until she became ill and he was forced to take public transportation. Her sales meeting for him each day was *"patience"* and *"persistence"*.

I hope if you ever get a chance to see this movie, you will. It was wonderful and inspiring! Do you love to sell?

The Difference Between Peddlers And Customer-Focused Sales People

If you are driven to win, you must stop peddling and start listening hard for the areas where you can make a difference in your client's business.

Michael was the top biller at the radio station we bought in the 80's. Hard sell/Zero concern for the client. When we took over the station I almost fired him. But, since he was the only one doing any billing (the station was a dog), I kept him, with the intention that I would fire him as soon as I got some decent sellers.

Mike was the old school sales person personified. When we'd put out a package at a sales meeting, Michael would head instantly to the copy machine and make 70 copies of our new package. In the next few days, he'd take it to everyone on his list. And he'd ask every one of them to buy.

Mike was the original hard charging closer. Always ask for the order. If the client said no once, it didn't bother Mike. He just brought them another package the next week. His drive was off the charts but his empathy skills were non-existent.

Mike did one thing right. He worked harder than anyone else did, and since he asked EVERYONE to buy, Mike wrote business. I hated his selling style. It was the opposite of everything I believed. But, because of Michael's work ethic he was effective. For three years, 1987-1989, Michael continued to be our top biller. Obviously, we didn't fire him!) Then the 1990 downturn hit. In less than 18 months, Michael's billing had crashed and he decided it was time to retire. Here's why. In a time of economic abundance, hard work and asking for the order, generates business.

What happens in a slowdown? Mike starved. In slower times, clients don't want packages; they want solutions to the problems their businesses face. The AE that provides them with solutions wins.

Remember the part of our UPGRADE training where I talk about the difference between Peddlers and the Customer Focused Sales Person? The Peddler (the package seller) gets hurt the most in an economic slowdown. There are so many "packages" available and so many peddlers going from account to account that peddlers struggle. The sales rep who succeeds is truly customer focused.

What kind of sales person are you?
- Do your clients consider you a peddler, or see you as an AE that actually gives a damn about them and their business?
- Are you there to take their money or are you one of the few who wouldn't ask for any money unless convinced it's good for the client?

There's a huge difference between the peddler and the customer focused AE. Customer focused AE's spends twice the amount of the time with a client in the needs analysis/diagnosis step because they are identifying the real hot button needs of a client.

Lots of sales people did OK in the last few years, even though they were peddlers. Times were good and ad money flowed more freely, but it's a new era now. If you are driven to win, you must stop peddling and start listening hard for the areas where you can make a difference in your client's business.

Finding Their Pain
The Clock Story

An AE told me about an example used by Walt Drissel, a sales professor at the University of Memphis. He was suggesting that sales people need to find a client's "pain," even when they don't see it themselves.

He used the following example:

A sales person was trying to sell a clock system to a movie theater with 12 screens. The clocks would indicate how much time was left before the show began. The cinema operator said they couldn't afford them. So, the salesperson developed the following scenario after studying the way customers behaved in the theater. It was as follows:

- ✓ 2 people per show skipped the concession stand because they thought they were late for the movie.
- ✓ Each person would spend about $6.00 at the concession stand.
- ✓ There are 12 screens at the theater.
- ✓ Each screen has four showings a day.
- ✓ There are 365 days a year.
- ✓ If that is the case, that equals $210,240.00 in lost concession stand revenue because people do not stop because they think they will be late for the movie.

- ✓ That makes the clock system an incredible investment.
- ✓ The salesperson made the sale.

This is a great example of finding a customer's "pain."

Taking Attorney Yellow Page Money - A Real Life Use Of The Clock Example

Misty Wages is an extremely effective AE at KLTV in Tyler, TX.* Misty was working with a personal injury lawyer. She had already signed a fairly significant UPGRADE and realized that if there were more dollars to be had, they would have to come from the Yellow Pages.

So, Misty developed an extensive phone call tracker for the law firm. She then produced regular reports that indicated the source of incoming phone calls and where, more importantly, cases came from.

The result? She was able to show the attorney that there was significant lack of impact from their Yellow Page advertising in certain directories. Not only did they get very few calls, they got even fewer cases. Therefore, those dollars might be better focused to increase frequency on her television campaign.

This is an extremely powerful way of demonstrating to a client whether or not certain advertising is working or not.

*Misty was promoted to LSM since this was originally written. This allows me to make a bigger point. There are AE's currently doing spectacular work! Maybe you are competing with them

The competitive bar is being raised and it is essential that we use ideas like this to help generate increases in client spending.

Think And Sell Like A CEO

Anthony Parinello wrote the book, *Selling to the V.I.T.O.* (Very Important Top Officer!) He thinks salespeople need to think and sell like CEO's. In his opinion, here are the 10 characteristics of top sales producers:

1) They are accountable for everything they say and do.

2) They recognize integrity as a dual edged sword. Not only must they tell the truth, they must also be willing to hear the truth.

3) They have confidence in themselves and they constantly reinforce that belief.

4) They put the client first.

5) They always strive to learn more, search for ways to improve themselves, develop their strengths and understand their weaknesses.

6) They are constantly trying to find ways to help others grow and develop. Generosity is returned multi-fold.

7) They are obsessed with progress. To them, progress means change and the opportunity it brings to move forward towards their goals.

8) When working with a prospect, they focus on the goals ("what needs to happen?") before getting distracted by the mechanics ("how will it happen?").

9) They make absolutely certain that they are an important part of the customer's solution and not part of the customer's problem.

10) They embrace new situations and actively look for new challenges.

Where are your improvement opportunities on this list?

How To Deal With Objections

Dealing With Objections

**There is only one real objection:
the client doesn't believe it will work.**

I used to spend a lot of time teaching AE's specifically how to deal with objections. Here is a step-by-step process. When you use it, you're ability to handle objections will grow quickly. Here is what I suggest:

Step One: Listen, completely, to the objection. Don't try to finish your clients' sentences for them.

Step Two: Repeat their objection back to them. Be sure to do that in a way that is not challenging or argumentative.

Step Three: Clarify the real issue. Here is what I say, *"I understand that you think our rates are too high, but let me ask you a question. If you were convinced, for the money we are talking about here, you would realize significant results, would you do it?"*

Using a sentence like this forces the client to zero in on the real objection. It isn't that the rates are too high; it isn't that you cover too broad an area, it isn't that you reach the wrong demo. It's ALWAYS that they don't believe it will work.

Step Four: Neutralize the Objection. Use success stories to demonstrate to the client that other people have dealt with this objection in the past. Use the great Dale Carnegie method: "I understand how you feel. Other people have felt the same way. What they have found is…"

By de-personalizing the objection and suggesting how other people have dealt with it, you communicate more effectively.

Step Five: Close. Summarize your answer to the objection and ask again for the order.

By using this step-by-step process, you will become more effective in dealing with objections. Most great sales people have to overcome three to four objections before they close a sale. If you are stopping after just one, you don't have the impact you should have compared to the time investment you have made.

"I'll Get Lost In The Clutter."

While traveling, I was watching the late news. This was a market that had an enormous number of car dealers advertising. (Many in this market had followed the lead of a hugely successful dealer who built his business with TV). Every break in the late news had a dealer in it. Some breaks had more than one. I could just hear a dealer in that market saying,

"I don't want to advertise there, it's too cluttered with other dealers."

How do you deal with that objection? Here are several ways:

Is it really cluttered? If 15 dealers are in the same program or on at the same time, that does not mean the viewer pays attention to all 15. After all, the #1 selling brand in America is Ford and they sell only 20% of the vehicles. Since we know that most people have already made up their minds what car to buy, a Ford dealer shouldn't care about the other 80%. No other ads EXCEPT <u>another</u> Ford dealer represent clutter to that dealer's ad.

Ask why it's cluttered.   Isn't the number of dealers advertising some indication of the results they are getting? TV, cable and radio aren't any more cluttered than the print ads the dealer uses. At least we try to keep competitive dealers away from each other.   The paper puts them right next to each other, so the customer can compare prices. The paper is nothing <u>but</u> clutter, and dealers believe that's a benefit. *"We have to have an ad in on Sunday, that's the big car day."*

Let me go back to the real objection: When a client says commercials are too cluttered, that is not their real objection. They are really telling you they are not convinced it will work.

<u>**I believe there is ONLY one real objection**</u>. Potential clients don't believe that, for the money you are asking, they will get huge results. You could spend a lot of time rebutting their point *("it's really not cluttered"* or *"everything is cluttered")* and, at the end, still not close a sale.   Why not respond by saying, *"yes...sometimes it is. That's because of how powerful it can be when it works. Your results will make you view the clutter as a minor nuisance, not an overwhelming problem."*   And then share some success stories. Don't chase the pretend objection. Deal with the real one and your sales will go up.

"Nobody Watches TV
In The Summer"

Have you ever heard that objection? If you haven't, it's only because you haven't made enough sales calls! Is it true? *Of course not.* But like many statements, it does have _some_ truth.

There's no question that certain time periods have less viewing during the summer months than they do in the dead of winter. People are spending more time outside. The days are longer. But, take a walk around your neighborhood any night around 9:30PM (some people call this walking the dog...I call it Market Research!) and notice the % of homes that have a TV on. In our neighborhood, that number is as high in summer as in the dead of winter. I've always believed that some time periods may do even better; early morning and late night, for instance. Have you noticed there are never re-runs on Soap Operas?

Here's what I say when a client brings up this subject:

1. **It's not true.** There is a switch in viewing habits and a decrease in some time periods.
2. **Even when viewing is down, it's still huge.** If TV viewing dropped by 20%, TV would still reach more people in our market every night than any other form of advertising.
3. **Prices usually drop as well.** That means advertisers can get a significant bump in frequency during the summer months, making ad results even stronger.
4. **But the real issue, Ms. Advertiser, is *can it get results?*** Then I share my favorite success story from a summer TV advertiser. I've got several because some of the biggest successes of my

TV career have been in the summer months when a client, who couldn't afford us in the winter, could use TV in the summer.

Like many objections we get in the selling process, you MUST be sure to understand the *real* question. *"Will it work for my business?"* Spend some time addressing the *real issue* by sharing success stories. If you don't, you can spend hours showing numbers that prove people do indeed watch TV in the summer, ONLY to lose the sale because you failed to deal with their real objection.

Do you get an indication yet that I feel VERY STRONGLY about this!

"Let Me Think About It"

You've made your fabulous proposal. You've asked for a lot of money AND the client seems interested. Then he says the killer phrase, ***"Let me think about it."*** How do you handle this?

This demands a two-part process. Part One is to immediately ask open-ended questions to determine if there is a specific problem or objection. I'll say, *"I appreciate why you'd want to do that. So I can be sure I've done my job, is there anything you feel that I haven't explained thoroughly enough, any questions, any area where you're planning to focus your thoughts??"*

I've never been a hard-charging closer. It's important to determine if there is a non-verbalized problem keeping them from making a decision right now.

I'll be honest. I am frequently asking clients for a lot of money and they don't make those decisions on the spot. I am required to come back at a later date and ask them if they have made up their mind. When that happens, remember to do the following:

- Whenever possible go back for your answer in person.
- Never ask if they've had a chance to think about it. They probably haven't.
- Re-energize them about your proposal. Try saying something like, *"After I left here last week, I wondered if I had spent enough time talking about how this part of our plan could help with your problem - opportunity. And when you add that to the ____ and the ____ and the ____ I really think this will help your company as it___. (What's in it for them.)*

Try this approach and I promise your closing percentage will go up.

"Newspaper Provides Instant Results …
TV Doesn't"

AE Question: I need a good answer to this. Car dealers say newspaper provides immediate results. TV ads do not. I know a lot of things to say, but I need the strongest concise response possible.

My Answer:

I can understand how you feel. Many dealers initially felt the same way, but here's what they found. When the creative and the frequency is RIGHT, you will see results this weekend. If you don't see results, it's because one of those two things is wrong. Please remember, TV also plants seeds for the buyer who will buy in 2 weeks or 2 months. It gives you far more impact for your money because it doesn't reach just the 'today' buyer.

That's why many of the most successful dealers in the country.....people like Ricart (The #1 Ford dealer in the US), Dubb Herring (selling over 300 cars per year in Picayune, Mississippi), and Earnharts use this approach.

Andy Mohr Ford uses TV only. He went from #8 in sales in Indianapolis to #1 in less than 9 months. Now he's #1 in the entire state of Indiana.

He does 24% of the Indianapolis Ford business with a less than great location. So if it's not working for you, then it's our job to see what's wrong to assure you get these kinds of results."

See what I've done?

- Acknowledge that the objection is valid.
- Let them know they are not alone.
- Tell them others originally felt the same way.
- <u>And share stories!!!</u>

"TV Didn't Score High."

"We took a survey of where people saw our ad. TV didn't score high."
When I hear this, I usually share a story. It's a true, real life story. I
encourage you to use it if you think it's helpful.

Several years ago, when I was a Sales Manager in Maine, a major client,
Blue Cross/Blue Shield, had a respected research company ask consumers
where they had seen Blue Cross advertising during the last few months.
The #1 answer was TV. This, despite the fact that Blue Cross *had not been
on TV in three years!!*

What should that say to you? That people don't have clue where they've
seen or read advertising. They don't sit by their television sets writing
down ads. They are relaxing, getting messages put in their head, maybe
even thinking about responding. By the next day, they don't have any clue
about where they saw it.

I usually tell a client that if I knew he was going to measure the schedule
through a survey, I would have done one of two things. I would have

included some outrageous copy point everybody would remember (be sure to mention Bill's big nose!!!), or pulled the ads, because I refuse to set myself up for failure in a test that is not relevant.

Be forceful about this, not apologetic. After all, research has proven the power of TV ads. There is only one way to judge the success of an ad campaign; what happened to traffic and sales during the time of the campaign? If it's up, Hurrah! - you've got an ad campaign that's working. If traffic is down, it still doesn't mean TV doesn't work. TV works! But that's when you check the copy and the frequency to insure you are maximizing the power of TV. (I hope you think of this when you sell it in the first place.)

When I ran radio stations, we would FORBID our AE's from allowing copy that said, "Mention this ad and get a free oil change with purchase." <u>Forbid it.</u> I'd ask the client how many times in their life they had ever done that. Most people never had themselves, so how could they expect their customers to do it?

Frankly, people don't like to admit they have been manipulated by advertising. That same customer often has no hesitation presenting a coupon, but they'll seldom mention an ad on TV or radio.

Why am I writing this? It's a reaction to the out-pouring of commentary predicting the demise of the TV business.

Want an example - how about a PBS segment on *"The News Hour with Jim Lehrer?"* While the piece did talk about the challenges to all advertising and did mention that the downturn in ad spending had especially impacted newspapers and magazines, the ad examples and much of the discussion was about the future of television advertising.

This is the reason for my concern. Your clients are seeing this kind of information; information that tells them that TV is hurting as an advertising medium. Some clients will be wondering if the decisions they are making are wrong.

It is essential that you have answers when your clients raise these questions. First the obvious rebuttals:

1. There is a 100-year tradition of pundits predicting that one media's rise would be the cause of another's demise. Radio was supposed to kill newspapers. Before that I suppose people predicted that newspapers would destroy posters. Today there are more posters than ever. Last time I checked, the newspaper was still going strong.

Radio was supposed to be gone by now, a victim of TV. After all, why would you listen to Jack Benny when you could hear and see him? So how's radio doing? Despite adding hundreds of additional choices in every market, it's billing more than ever.

TV was supposed to be hurt by Cable. Cable was supposed to be chased away by satellite dishes. TiVO is going to kill those. Now, the Internet will mean the end of it all!

And yet, as new media arrive, competition forces the current players to get better. No one appears to die, and if they are dying, it sure is a very slow process.

2. Look at this year's Upfront. That's the period where all the major national companies make commitments for the following TV season. (This occurs in June each year.) The predictions were that upfront was supposed to be bad, really bad; maybe even a drop in the commitments from what happened last year. So what happened?   Upfront money soared. It was huge. Marketing sages may be saying that TV is dying, but the people who need to sell their products are voting with their money, and there are no signs of death. In fact, the patient seems healthier than ever at the moment.

3. Ditto the commitments to the Cable Networks. Their Upfront comes after the networks. In a word - it has been great.

In that PBS story, there is an interview with the head of Ford marketing. He talks about moving money to events like concert sponsorships to reach consumer groups that are hard to find. A local client may think their money might be better spent if they sponsored the local road race or Little League team. Nothing could be further from the truth! What the PBS piece doesn't mention is the single largest part of Ford's budget goes to _____! You guessed it. It's the same TV that the piece said is dying.

If I am Ford and I have billions to spend, what's a little spent on concerts, or promotion or product placement. But when a local client does that, what happens? They waste their money and totally diminish their impact.

By the way....here's a quick quiz. What company sponsored the last big concert you went to? Can't remember? I sure can't. You know why? No frequency! That's why promotion or product placement can serve only as the icing on the cake. It's not strong enough to be the cake.

4. The PBS piece reminded people of a time when TV ads became part of the culture. They played a bit from the Alka Seltzer commercials. Remember *"I can't believe I ate the whole thing"*? They suggested that kind of impression doesn't happen today. Oh yeah? Have you ever heard anyone say *"Whasssup?"* Been anywhere where people have mimicked the AFLAC duck? This is a fabulous TV campaign that put a decades-old company on the map. But TV is dead. That's not supposed to happen anymore. I forgot!

5. And what about the audience? What are they doing? They're simply watching more TV each and every year. Recent numbers projected TV viewing by household through 2006 and guess what? Viewing is projected to grow every year

6. The best rebuttal of all, whenever a client is questioning you on the validity of your product, is to share success stories. *"I don't know about*

152

those national trends but don't tell Joe's Furniture that TV is dying. They just had the biggest month in their history." "And the same with ___ and ___, and ___." Bury this baloney in an avalanche of success stories. Success stories are the most powerful antidotes to misinformation.

Don't think that I am a Pollyanna, blindly supporting a business in the absence of facts. Nothing could be further from the truth. I believe that TV and Cable have changed and will continue to change. We will learn more about getting results for clients. We'll learn that some of the ways we got results years ago won't work today.

20 years ago I sold TV schedules with broad rotators. Lots of reach, and in a 3-4 station environment, probably got some frequency as well. Today I'd never do that. We sell local clients on the idea of dominating a TV program or day-part.

When I first worked in cable, it was common to insert on *"the wheel"*. A random, run-them-anywhere approach to scheduling, inserted on 4-5 networks. Today cable systems can help advertisers pick the networks or shows that best target their prospects.

It's the same thing with creative. In his wonderful *14 Rules of the Guru* seminar on creating ads that sell, my colleague, Don Fitzgibbons, shows ad after ad that didn't work. He shows audiences how to make ads produce results for businesses. He reminds me that I used to say *"even bad TV ads work"*. That's not true anymore. We must get better at running effective commercials.

So we've changed and we'll continue to change. But one thing hasn't changed. That's the power of TV.

Need one last piece of proof? Political clients, who have only one chance to make a sale, will spend millions of dollars on advertising. Where will 90% of it go? You know the answer. Why? Talk to any candidate who has been the victim of an attack ad. Ask them if they think TV works.

One More Time:
There Is Only One REAL Objection

The client says...

- *"Your rates are too high."*
- *"You cover too broad an area."*
- *"I tried it before and it did not work."*
- *"You do not reach my customer."*

What are they really saying??

For a long, long time, I have believed there is only one *real* objection. That is the client believing, *"it won't work."* The client is really saying that the results won't justify the expense. <u>That</u> is the only *real* objection!

That objection may be gift wrapped in lots of ways. Your rates are too high; you cover too broad an area, etc. Many sales people make the mistake of chasing the gift-wrapping by responding –

> *"We really are not expensive."*

> *"We don't cover too broad of an area."*

The real issue is they *doubt* the results. Don't spend all of your time in the sales process answering fake objectives. Deal with the real one. Go after their *perception* that it might not work and *deal* with that.

One way is to say to the client, *"Well, I know you think our rates are too high but let me ask you a question. If you believed that you would get spectacular results for the amount of money we were talking about, would you do it?"*

I will guarantee you the answer is *yes*, and when you hear it, you will know what the real problem is.

BUILDING SUCCESSFUL
BUSINESS RELATIONSHIPS

Your Relationship With Key Accounts

Let me start with a story.

Last week, I received a phone call from one of our Achievers Circle members. He wanted my help. One of his largest accounts just switched agencies and the new agency was not particularly friendly to his medium. What should he do?

My first question was, *"What is your relationship with the economic buyer at the client location?"* He replied, *"I really don't have one."*

At that point, although we spoke a little longer, there was not really a lot I could advise him to do. I can make you a promise - every agency will get fired. No agency keeps accounts forever. The day an agency gets fired by one of your KEY accounts is the day you may discover the penalty of not having a relationship directly with the client.

Here is what I believe...

Every six weeks the following ought to occur with your KEY Accounts:

1)   They should receive a handwritten thank you from you.

2)   They should receive an article about their business.

3)   They should receive a phone call or letter from one of your managers that says thank you. (80% of a manager's contacts with KEY Accounts ought to be temperature taking and thank you's.)

4)   Three to four times each year, every KEY Account should receive something extra from you. Drop in with a pizza during a promotion, volunteer to put on a sales meeting for their team, sponsor a sales contest, or offer to send letters to KEY customers about their advertising.

This is so easy to put off. I know because I do it myself. It is easy to postpone because there is zero penalty in this month's billing. If you don't send thank you notes this month, it won't cost you a dime - this month. What will it cost you, eventually? It will cost you the opportunity to significantly change the nature of your relationship with this client one year from today.

I believe one of the things that distinguishes the very best sales people from most of us in our business is their effectiveness at setting aside the time to *"build bridges"* to their KEY Accounts. They schedule some time each week – or each month – to specifically engage in bridge building because they understand how important it is.

Stephen Covey called this Quadrant Four work. This is work that is important – but not urgent. Many of us spend a lot of our time doing the things that are urgent – but not important. **Really successful people understand what is important and make time for it.**

There is another step in the process of building relationships with KEY Accounts. I urge you to not only go after the low hanging fruit.

We all have clients who are more accessible than others. They don't mind the contact. They have an agency that doesn't get upset, and they are open to your thank you's and drop-ins. Because they are more accessible, we are tempted to spend more time with them. Don't ignore them, but spend some time looking at the balance of your KEY Accounts with a goal of building excellent relationships with them.

Here is what I urge you to do this week:

1) Write down every one of your KEY Accounts. Honestly assess where your relationship is with them today, and where you need it to be.

2) Do you have a relationship with the <u>right</u> person?

3) What is your plan to develop a good relationship? Do you need to write thank you notes, send articles, or have your manager get in contact with this client?

4) When are you going to take these steps?

Remember, the principal characteristic that distinguishes the real stars in our business is the quality of their relationship with their largest accounts.

The KEY Account principle is based on the 80/20% Rule. But, it occurs to me that there is another derivative of the 80/20% Rule. If you spend 80% of your time with just 20% of your KEY Accounts, that causes you to think you are aggressive at building relationships with KEY Accounts, while a large percent are left with no contact.

Build a great relationship with every one of your KEY Accounts! Try to grow the relationship with the economic buyer wherever and whenever possible.

If asked about your relationship with your Key Account, don't ever have to say, "I really don't have one."

Going Around The Agency
And Living To Talk About It

AE's MUST build relationships directly with the client
WHENEVER that is possible.

I know that makes a lot of AE's nervous. In fact, a group I worked with a recently was quite vocal about how I had nudged their comfort zones pretty significantly. Interestingly, three were former media buyers who were quick to acknowledge how little real authority they had when they were with agencies.

Here's what you need to do to be aggressive and still keep your relationship with the agency strong.

- **Deliver extraordinary service to the agency.** Be their best AE. This is your insurance policy when (not if!) you do something that bugs them.

- **Go to the client when everything is going great.** If you wait until you are off a buy or your share is not what you wanted, you will be perceived as a whiner. Start to build the bridges while things are good, with small gestures that help you stand out. Thank you notes and articles sent to the real client, the economic buyer, are best. **Repeat after me…the time to go to the client is when everything is going GREAT!!**

- **Speaking of thank you's, I believe that 70% of your contact**

with the client ought to be "thank you's" or articles. Build the bridge first, then walk over it!

- **Get your managers involved**. Generals talk to Generals. Ask your Sales Manager or GM to make a call to the economic buyer of the client. And when they call, the goal is to have them say *"Thank you"* or ask *"How are we doing for you?"* or *"Is there anything else we can do to serve you?"*

- **When you meet with the client in person, do diagnosis first.** Learn about their needs and their issues. Don't pitch your product the first time you meet the client.

- **Look for opportunities to <u>add value</u> to the relationship**. Offer to have their sales meeting at your facility. Talk about providing contest prizes for a promotion they are doing. We are show business and we can use that to add some magic to their operation.

In another chapter, I wrote about taking one hour per week, actually scheduling it in your PDA or Daytimer, and using that hour to solidify relationships with your KEY Accounts. <u>Nothing you can do will be more profitable.</u>

A sales manager, who worked for me, introduced me to the idea that one must have a relationship directly with the account. I will confess it challenged my comfort zone. Today, I am convinced it is an absolute necessity, but sometimes AE's think I am advocating heading straight out to the client with the 'package of the week.' Wrong! Head out to the client to build bridges. Take one hour a week to do the steps outlined above and you will be so much further ahead of other AE's who compete with you on this account. That's the strategy of a winner.

Owning Your Key Accounts

I spent a few hours with the person I think is the best AE in America. He's Achievers Circle member, Randy Watson, from WTHR in Indianapolis. We spent some time together while Randy was in Florida on vacation and then made a sales call together on a dealer in Indianapolis. It was great to have time in the car with Randy.

Many of you have heard me speak about Randy at seminars. What he does has taught me a lot about what great AE's can do to separate themselves from the competition. I'm convinced that one of the most important things you must do – *today* - is build trust with your clients. Randy is the model of just how to do that.

Randy's big thing? Articles! He may be the best-read sales person I have ever met. I'm a voracious reader, but he has me beat. It's what he does with the info that sets him apart.

If you are a KEY account of Randy's (both agency and, more importantly, a client), chances are you'll get a copy of an article that is relevant to your business many, many times in the course of the year.

Randy will send out literally dozens of articles each and every week. I know. I'm blessed to be on his list for some of them. He makes a major commitment of his time to do this. **What does he get back for his investment?**

First, he gets remembered. There are nine account executives at WTHR. I worked with them during large, company-wide sales conferences. A year ago, I was going to Indy to work just with Randy's group. I realized that he was the only name I knew. How had he done that? By sending me articles. He had worked my own seminar on me. Let me ask, aren't you always one of nine or more AE's from different media trying to get thru to a client? Think about getting remembered; it works.

Second, Do you think the person who does that separates himself from all the AE's who call on this client? Don't you think the client will feel Randy is someone who can be trusted?

Third...and this is just my opinion...that trust leads to Randy being able to meet with the client and do a Time Out Call. I believe that's the major goal of the bridge building process.

How effective is this? One number might tell you. Randy personally billed over $1 million dollars in the Olympics that year. Impressed? I am, but even better, almost every dime of it was sold before last July, and it all stuck after September 11th.

Articles aren't the only thing Randy does. A realtor friend of mine joined Randy and me for golf in Florida. Randy sent him a thank you note and passed this realtor's name on to a family member that buys investment real estate here. (If Randy even remotely sensed that he might be buying Indianapolis TV advertising, my friend is probably already starting to receive articles!)

Here's the bottom line. Would you spend ONE hour each week in activities that build the bridge to your biggest clients? Writing thank you notes - sending articles - getting your manager to call to say thanks - researching challenges and opportunities in their category?

If you spent just one hour weekly, maybe the last thing you do each Friday, you will be among the *elite* in our business. Maybe someday I'll be writing about you. Thanks Randy, for letting me share your not-so-secret ideas. We've all heard them before. It's *doing* them that counts.

A Great KEY Account Idea

Brad Streit is the VP/GM of our TV client in Tyler, TX, KLTV. He has a great idea to solidify relationships with KEY Accounts.

Once a month, Brad takes the station's weekly, department-head meeting off-site at a key account business' location. What a great opportunity for all the managers to build better relationships with their KEY Accounts and to say thank you in a very special way.

I love this idea. I think it makes a huge statement to our clients and can definitely have real impact.

CUSTOMER SERVICE

I received a personal lesson from a powerful teacher on how to stand out from the crowd.

Before our Boot Camp, I was talking to speakers about what they might bring to the program we were doing for Sales Managers, and I'd watched a lot of demo tapes to judge talent. All were good. Very good.

One of the speakers we contacted, T. Scott Gross, wrote the best-ever book on customer service, *Positively Outrageous Service*.

When FedEx arrived with Scott's "kit", it had all the usual components - wonderful letters from past audiences, a list of topics. But Scott's kit had a few other surprises.

Scott had included two "Nutrageous" candy bars: (rhymes with Outrageous ...get it?) He'd autographed a copy of his newest book for me. There was also some silliness. His brother is Scott's marketing director and his card says he's "the younger and better looking brother."

Then we played his demo tape. Who came on first? Scott. He had a personal greeting for me and also for Cheryl, my assistant, who had phoned him. At this point I'm saying, "WOW!!"

We had called their office at 3PM the day before! They had recorded the customized opening - edited to their normal demo - and had it ready to be sent by Fed Ex.

Scott had done just a few little gestures (candy bar, humor, book and personalized video), but he had instantly let me know that he's an 'above and beyond' type person.

The demo was incredible. It had a wonderful mix of humor and content. Did it sell me? I had already hired a speaker by the time Scott's material arrived, but now I had two speakers. That morning, I put together a deal to include Scott as part of our conference.

Are there lessons here? I hope so. Scott Gross demonstrates three, all of which are important:

1. His entire attitude is "How can I serve you?" I find that servant mentality to be a big part of many achievers.

2. His little extra's separate him from everyone else.

3. He delivers on his promise. He's good. After all - if you love the waitress but the food stinks, you don't go back.

What are you doing to stand out from the crowd?

Lagniappe is a Cajun word. It describes the *"little bit extra."* It is the 13th donut in the dozen, or the tie that gets thrown in when you buy the suit. It is the seller's way of saying, "I want to give you everything you expect and *a little bit more."*

2003 RAB keynoter, Les Brown, said it a different way. He said if you want to be successful *"Work harder than they pay you for."*

I had a peak experience at dinner in New Orleans. The restaurant was Commander's Palace. I had been told it was one of New Orleans best restaurants. The food did not disappoint. In fact, the meal was as good as I have had in the last several years.

What really set Commander's Palace apart was Wendall. Wendall was our waiter. The service was the best I have ever experienced in any restaurant. (Trust me...I'm an expert in this category. Because of my travel life, I eat out way too much!). What did Wendall do?

First, he had a total attitude of warmth and desire to assure we had a great time. This started when he introduced himself to us and set the agenda for how the evening was going to be. Each time Wendall returned to the table, he called my colleague by name. He knew his name because he had made the reservation for dinner. His service was friendly, even joking with us occasionally. (T. Scott Gross says that great customer service can often involve *"playing"* with the customer.) Then, the *"Lagniappe."* Both of us had ordered desserts and when he brought them, he said they were his gift to us for our first time at the restaurant.

Do you think Wendall earned more than a standard gratuity? He did more than he was paid for, but ended up being paid very well.

To seal the deal, when we told him we thought the service was extraordinary, he whipped out a business card for each of us. He said he would be thrilled if we asked for him when we came back to Commander's Palace. And, I will - ask for him <u>and</u> go back to Commander's Palace.

When I did customer service seminars, I would say, *"Nobody remembers <u>good</u> service."* There are only two kinds of customer service that we remember. First is bad service. We <u>do</u> remember that. The other service we remember is <u>outstanding service</u>.

Many of us think we give our customers good service, and we probably do. Wendall inspires me about how much more impact we can have when we just do just a *"little bit more."*

What is the level of customer service you are providing to your customers?

A Great Selling Story

Amy Bobchek is a Regional Manager for Adelphia Cable. She forwarded this to me. It is an extremely powerful story about the effectiveness of going one step beyond. As I read it, I couldn't help but think that every Achiever I know does just a little bit more than other AE's. That little bit can have a huge impact. *You may want to pass this story on to some of your car dealer clients.*

Yesterday, my husband and I went to Pohanka Lexus to look at cars. The lot was rather busy as one might expect on a weekend with great weather. We were looking around at cars when a salesman approached us and we spoke with him about the car we wanted. After looking at the selection available, we settled on a car we liked and said we'd like to drive it and possibly start negotiating. He said he was sorry, but that wasn't possible. Puzzled, I asked why, and he responded, "Oh, we're closed on Sundays."

This salesman had decided to spend his Sunday at the lot, developing prospects, despite the fact that it was closed. Remember, I said the lot was very busy. Virtually everyone who set foot on that lot yesterday got his personal attention and his card. Imagine how many cars he's going to sell!

By the way, he sat in his car between chats with people. He was driving a brand-new Lexus with personalized (not dealer) plates. He's obviously doing a lot of things right!

What will you do today to set yourself apart from every other sales person in the universe?

REMEMBER:

If you just want to make money selling advertising,

- focus on just making sales.

But if you want a fulfilling career,

filled with incredible opportunities

and lots of personal AND financial rewards,

- make a difference.

The Achievers Circle Membership

Exclusive for Account Executives Only!
Membership is limited

Here's just a sampling of what you'll get....

- ✓ Achievers Circle Membership and Personal Subscription to *Auto Revenue Insights* Newsletter

- ✓ A Welcome Kit including your own personal copy of all of our revenue growth tools, including, *The Power of Focus*, and *UPGRADE Selling*™

- ✓ Quarterly "Members Only" telephone Seminars on timely business topics to help you excel

- ✓ Every 60 days a "members Only' Call In Day with Jim Doyle answering selling or marketing questions

- ✓ Instant E-Mail Updates with critical information AE's need

- ✓ Weekly informational E-Mails sharing sales ideas, sales training or critical information AE's need

To Learn More, go to:

www.upgradeselling.com/achieverscircle/

About Jim Doyle

Jim Doyle is President of Jim Doyle and Associates. His company works with television stations whose managers expect far more than average revenue growth and want to prepare their sales teams for success in a future of tremendous change. Jim's UPGRADE Selling™ system is the street-proven way AE's build partnerships with advertisers and significantly grow revenue.

Jim's a unique trainer and management consultant: he still makes sales calls! It keeps him current and keeps his seminars very real world. His thought-provoking programs offer techniques, tools and solutions that lead quickly to revenue growth. Jim believes that "training without action is just entertainment."

Jim has presented his marketing workshop for advertisers, *Prospering in Mega Competitive Times*, in more than 350 cities over the past 11 years. He's the author of numerous audio and video programs, including *UPGRADE Selling™, The Power of Focus* and *TV: The Dealer's Edge.*
Jim is a columnist for a national trade publication and the publisher of a monthly newsletter about the car business, written for advertising sales people. His National Auto Satellite Conferences have had the largest audience of any conferences of their kind. Jim is a member of the National Speakers Association.

Jim began his broadcasting career as a TV sales rep in Portland, Maine. During 30+ years in advertising and broadcasting, he has owned an advertising agency, been Director of Sales for a TV station group, and

General Manager/ part owner of a radio station. Jim has served as Chair of the TV-B Sales Training Committee. He started teaching sales in the mid-70's, returning to training and management consulting full-time in 1991.

Jim lives in Sarasota, Florida.